Best wishes, Herman Linder

67th Birthday Gift
From Jackie & Lyle Omstead

TURN HIM LOOSE!

TURN HIM LOOSE!

Herman Linder, Canada's Mr. Rodeo

by
Cliff Faulknor

Western Producer Prairie Books
Saskatoon, Saskatchewan

Cover design by Jean MacGregor

Printed in Canada by
Modern Press

 1

Saskatoon, Saskatchewan

Canadian Cataloguing in Publication Data
Faulknor, Cliff, 1913-
   Turn him loose!

   Includes index.
   ISBN 0-919306-81-0 bd.
   ISBN 0-919306-82-9 pa.

   1. Linder, Herman. 2. Rodeos. 3. Cowboys - Canada - Biography. I. Title.

GV1833.6.L55F38   79.8   C77-002123-9

To rodeo cowboys everywhere

CONTENTS

FOREWORD

The name Herman Linder has been synonymous with rodeo for nearly half a century, and well it should be. Rodeo is a sport, a business, a form of entertainment, and a way of life. As you will discover in this biography, no person has put his mark on all facets of rodeo as indelibly as Herman Linder.

As a contestant, Linder was a superb rodeo athlete, competing in every event in rodeo, and winning, during the 1920s and 30s, an unparalleled twenty-two championships at the Calgary Stampede alone. In today's terminology he was a superstar.

As one of the founders and spokesmen of the Cowboy Turtle Association in 1936, the first organization of rodeo cowboys, he was one of the architects of the present structure of rodeo. Both the Professional Rodeo Cowboys' Association, Denver, and the Canadian Rodeo Cowboys' Association have grown out of the concept conceived by the Turtles.

In addition to being a superior rodeo athlete and a builder of the sport, Linder was also the originator and producer of some of the most highly regarded professional rodeos in Canada, including the major rodeo presented in conjunction with Expo 67 in Montreal.

Throughout his career as a contestant, an organizer, and a producer, and throughout his life, Herman Linder has epitomized the highest ideals of Western conduct. He was humble in victory and gracious in defeat; straightforward and honest in his dealings, his word always being as good as his bond; courteous, generous, and kind to all. In short, he is a gentleman. The rodeo world is extremely proud of Herman Linder the cowboy, and Herman Linder the man.

The written record of the sport of rodeos is woefully short. This biography of a man whose career parallels the development of the sport over the last fifty years could not be more appropriate.

The book is authentic, provocative and highly entertaining, as is its subject. I commend it to you.

BERRY TIBBITT
Secretary-Manager
Canadian Rodeo Cowboys' Association

ACKNOWLEDGMENTS

In gathering material for this book I received help from many sources. I wish to thank Mrs. Georgeen Barrass, Assistant Chief Archivist of the Glenbow-Alberta Institute for her help in procuring many photos, especially the photograph of the famous "Barn Scene". The *Calgary Herald,* the Calgary Exhibition and Stampede Association, the Edmonton Exhibition Association and the American Legion Rodeo, Sidney, Iowa, all contributed photos. I am indebted to Lionel and Mae Humphreys of West Vancouver for their research efforts at the Vancouver Library, to the work of all those early newspaper reporters who covered the rodeo scene, in particular, the writings of Dorothy Weyman, Boston, Mass., and Viscount Castlerosse, London, England. I am also indebted to Alberta Culture for a grant which enabled me to take time off to write this book; to my wife, Betty, who did the typing; to Warner Linder for his recollections; and of course, to Herman and Agnes Linder for their unfailing cooperation and hospitality.

CLIFF FAULKNOR

CHAPTER ONE

ALBERTA PEARL

Alberta Pearl was her name and bronco busting was her game, but she didn't know it was her game yet. All the slim, fourteen-year-old in the faded middy blouse, short skirt, and outsize sheepskin chaps could see was the six-dollar prize which awaited her if she could stay on the hurricane deck of the bronc for eight seconds. And six dollars was a mighty big sum to the Cardston youngster in 1921.

As she took up her position above the chute, the crowd gasped and leaned for a closer look. A young girl as a bronco buster? What was the world coming to? Pearl's teacher, who never missed a rodeo or ended a sentence with a preposition, wondered to what was the world coming. Even Old Chief Mountain, peering grandly down on the scene through a fleece of summer clouds must have stood aghast at this brash intrusion into the male domain.

But Pearl was more worried about the floppy hat anchored tightly under her determined chin by a broad ribbon, than about the surcingle-rigged outlaw that snorted and fidgeted below her. Another concern was the crowd itself from whom she kept her face averted, until she had to concentrate all her attention on the bronc.

Outwardly calm, she waited for just the right moment to slip down onto the squirming back. This would be her first ride in a rodeo contest, but not her first time on the back of a bucking horse — not by a long shot. She had been riding buckers since she was twelve years old.

The right moment came and she slipped easily down. The bronc gave a heave as it felt her weight then became strangely quiet as if saving its strength for the contest to come. Suddenly she heard the announcer's voice, bellowing her chute number, her name, and the name of her horse. She didn't even notice that his announcement ended with a chuckle.

Pearl felt the bronc's muscles starting to bunch under her as she cried "Turn him loose!" to the chute gateman. On protesting hinges, the gate swung open and with one jump the bronc was out into the arena. He squealed and jumped again, and daylight showed under the woolly chaps as Pearl rose briefly skyward. But she was still on when those hooves returned to Mother Earth.

The crowd roared its appreciation.

Then the bronc headed off across the infield like an arthritic jackrabbit, squealing and grunting its anger at every hop. Every time those hooves hit the dirt, Pearl felt the contact all the way to her teeth, but she increased the pressure of her legs against the sweaty flanks and stayed with him.

The horse sunfished a couple of times and the roar of the crowd deepened. Pearl wasn't sure whether they were cheering for her or the bronc.

She had become attuned to the outlaw's plunges now and could feel that six-dollar prize almost within her grasp. Then all at once it changed tactics and began to whirl around and around in a tight circle. Pearl felt herself getting a little dizzy, but she hung in there grimly. She had come too far to give in now.

Suddenly the horn blared and she knew she had made it. She heard the thunder of hooves and pick-up man Dud Leavitt rode up beside the plunging bronc and reached out a helping hand. As Pearl swung up behind him, another rider chased the bronc off to a corral gate at the end of the field.

"Hey, where are you going?" Pearl cried in alarm as Leavitt headed towards the grandstand instead of back to the chutes.

"I'm going to show you off to the crowd," he grinned. "Not often they get a chance to see a girl bronc rider!"

"In a pig's eye!" snorted Pearl, attempting to slip off the saddle horse and gain the safety of the ground.

Every time Leavitt swung his horse around so the crowd could get a look at her face, Pearl would turn her face the other way.

"She sure is a bashful one," she heard somebody shout from the grandstand.

Finally, Leavitt rode back to the chutes in disgust. Pearl slid gratefully to the ground and ran behind the chutes to change.

"I just couldn't get those clothes off fast enough," Herman Linder laughed as he recalled his first rodeo performance. "That was the first and last time I ever dressed up as a girl. It was a stunt, you see. The people running the Cardston Rodeo figured the crowd wouldn't recognize me dressed as a girl and they knew I could handle myself on a bucking horse."

Many years later when Herman had become an established rider, rodeo buffs would come up to him and ask if he recalled a famous girl bronc rider named "Alberta Pearl" and how well she could ride, little realizing they were talking to "Pearl" in the flesh.

"Sure, she could ride well," chuckled Warner Linder, Herman's older brother. "When we were kids, Herman and I lived to ride. We started riding yearling steers when we were ten to eleven years old. By the time we were twelve, we were trying our hand at bucking horses."

"That's a long time ago," Herman nodded, "over fifty years, in fact. I suppose that first bronc had a name, but I don't remember what it was.

"In those days, they didn't have strings of horses that went around the rodeo circuit like they do today," he explained. "They'd bring in these horses — wild horses, I guess you'd call them — right off the range, although, at that time, they did have local horses with a great reputation without being what you'd call top bucking horses. If they had names they were probably made-up names for each particular rodeo."

Later on, when he had become a big name on the North American circuit, Herman was to meet and conquer bucking horses that had become famous in their own rights with colorful names such as: Broomtail, Liberty Bond, Blondie, Black Cat, Miss Meeks, Old Man of the Mountain, Too Bad, and Easy Money. And, to this day, he swears they made so little impression on him he cannot remember one from the other.

There are always exceptions, of course, and two come readily to mind. For instance, old Pardner almost nipped Herman's career in the bud by bucking him off so easily and often he began to despair of ever being a bronc rider. Then there was Rimrock, who threw rodeo promoter Linder for a financial loss and bucked him all the way to B.C.'s Supreme Court. A man isn't likely to forget a pair of horses like that.

Two years after "Alberta Pearl's" first encounter with rodeo, Herman entered a professional rodeo contest in his own right and won it. For ten years the 145-pound champion strode across the rodeo scene like a giant with seven-league boots. He travelled to Australia to display his skills at the Royal Agricultural Fair at a huge arena in Sydney, winning silver cups both times for the individual top score in saddle bronc riding. He went to England and won right up until the penultimate day when he stepped off a non-bucker and turned his ankle which put him out of the finals.

Despite the protests of promoters and fellow riders alike, Herman decided to hang up his competition saddle in 1938. He was thirty-one years old, and in his opinion, he had been sitting the hurricane deck long enough. He made his last ride in Madison Square Garden that year to the roar of thousands of fans and came off with top money. They liked him so well they asked him back the next year to judge the big event. His final competition ride came that same year.

Herman Linder wasn't just a bronco rider. In addition to saddle bronc and bareback titles, he won honors in bull riding, wild steer riding, and calf roping. Although he never won what is officially known as a World Title, he was Canadian All-Around Champion seven times and North American All-Around Champion five times and the latter event was open to anyone in the world.

He first sprang into prominence at the Calgary Stampede in 1929 when he took the Canadian championship away from all-time great Pete Knight. In nine years of competition at Calgary, Herman won an incredible total of twenty-two championships. Little wonder that headlines in Canadian newspapers of those days ran stories that proclaimed him "The Cowboy Supreme" and "King of the Cowboys!"

Said the *Calgary Herald,* Saturday, July 14th, 1934: "Turning in one of the greatest individual performances in the history of the Calgary Stampede, Herman Linder, youthful cowboy from Cardston, Alberta, won the Canadian Bronc Riding Championship with Saddle, the Bareback Bucking Horse Riding Championship, the Wild Steer Riding Championship, in addition to placing himself second in the North American Bronc Riding Championship with Saddle in the finals Saturday afternoon . . . .Linder was declared Best All-Around Cowboy for the fourth consecutive year."

When the big rodeo show at Sidney, Iowa, celebrated its Fiftieth Anniversary in 1973, the American Legion post which sponsored it put out a book describing how the show got started and naming the big-time rodeo stars who had competed there over the years. In the history of their event, said the book, two cowboys had dominated the competitions: before World War II, it was Herman Linder of Cardston, Alberta, and afterwards it was Jim Shoulders of Henrietta, Oklahoma.

As Herman's fame grew, so did the headlines. Screamed a big heading in an American paper, "Linder

Man of the Year At National Cowboy Hall of Fame!"
Shouted another: "Herman Linder Crowned Rodeo
King!" And yet another: "Cardston Rodeo Hero Invited to
World's Fair!"

Years later, after he had quit riding and become a
rodeo promoter, Herman Linder made headlines in the big
dailies of Vancouver, B.C. for the better part of a year,
more often than not in two-inch type. These screamers
were of a radically different flavor, but that is a story in
itself.

CHAPTER TWO

THE MUSIC OF HORSES' HOOVES

What makes a champion cowboy? Linder says he doesn't know, but he figures a bronc buster is born, not made. Some say it's a combination of an athlete's coordination and the sense of balance of a tightrope walker. And they could be right, because Herman's father was an acrobat in Switzerland and before he came to America, and his act included tightrope walking.

Herman Linder senior was born in a small town in the Alps. When he grew to young manhood he joined an athletic club there and set his mind on becoming an expert gymnast and tumbler. Later he got a job as a tightrope walker and acrobat in a travelling circus and started to tour the country. Finally he grew tired of circus life and, with his wife Marie, emigrated to the United States where his older brother had already become established in Wisconsin. Here he proceeded to learn Swiss cheese making, something he had never bothered to do at home.

Young Herman was born in Darlington, Lafayette County, Wisconsin, August 5th, 1907. A short while later, his father moved the family about twenty miles across the state line to Stockton, Illinois, where he set himself up in the cheese business, buying all his milk from local farmers.

"When World War I came along, Dad's business began to pick up," said Herman, "and as usually happens in wartime, he made quite a little money in a short space of time. But not enough to buy himself a farm in that country, which was what he really wanted."

Land around Stockton was selling for $200 to $300 an acre then. Not too many of the land-hungry immigrants could raise so much in those days, so the railroads — both American and Canadian — were advertising for people to head out West where land was much cheaper. After a while, these glowing ads got to Linder senior and he decided to make a move.

"Moving was a heartbreaking event," Herman Linder recalled. "People in that Illinois town really liked Dad and he liked them. When it came time to leave, a farmer friend named Will Bonvour drove us to the train station in an old Surrey buggy with fenders on the wheels, front and rear, and a roof with curtains. He even offered to send the money to come home if things didn't work out. Along the way, school children waved goodbye to us.

"So we left with tears in our eyes," Herman continued, "but it didn't take us children long to get over it, especially my brother Warner and I. As a matter of fact, both of us were looking forward to coming out West because now we figured we'd get a chance to see some cowboys and Indians and ride horses. We were crazy to get riding even then."

Herman and Marie Linder and their four children landed at Cardston in the spring of 1918. They bought a section of land about six miles south of town, not far from the U.S. border. The eldest child was their daughter, Minnie, and the youngest was daughter, Leona, who was only a year and a half at the time. The boys, Warner and Herman, were in the middle. For The first day or two, the family stayed at the Cahoon Hotel to give themselves a chance to get their bearings.

"When we landed in Cardston, things were a lot different than they are today," Herman recalled. "All you could hear outside the hotel was the rattle of wagons and the sound of horses' hooves. It was like music to us!

Warner and I would rush to the window and gape at the cowboys coming in with their fancy boots, woolly chaps, and big hats. What a thrill that was! We vowed someday we'd get ourselves outfits just like that."

The family moved out to the farm on the 1st of April. Just to make things nice and cosy for them, there had been a bit of a snowfall the night before. The buildings on the place were a far cry from the splendid buildings on the Linder spread today. Only a little log cabin remains of the original structures and it's in a lot better shape now than it was then.

"That log cabin didn't even have a shingled roof on it," Herman smiled at the recollection. "Warner and I slept in there and we had an umbrella over our heads to keep the snow and rain off us. Even the folk's home was just a two-room shack, really. That was one of the most disappointing things we found here because back in Illinois the people had such fine houses."

The year 1918 proved to be a very dry year and the winter which followed was practically snowless. When 1919 came in, the sun-bleached land was as dry as a keg of powder and just as ready to blow.

"It was probably the driest spell this part of the country has seen in the fifty-seven years we've been in Canada," said Herman. "Dad had bought some cattle at $100 a head and a good team for $500 to $600, so we came into the fall of 1919 with no feed. Being green at this game, Dad did like everybody else who was in the same boat. He kept the stock and got feed that was being brought in. By the spring of 1920, hay was selling for fifty dollars a ton."

Linder senior mortgaged his farm and borrowed money wherever he could just to keep going. Then, in May, along came that nemesis of all foothills cattlemen, the late spring snowstorm, and most of the cattle in the country perished. As a result, everybody was broke — even the big cattle outfits. Linder let half of his section go, keeping only the half with the buildings which forms the core of the 1,600-acre Linder ranch today. For a while, it became more of a mixed farm than a livestock operation.

Young Herman can remember a Christmas when the family was so broke the only present under the tree was a doll sent by an Uncle for little Leona. They made a Santa Claus mask for his father and also decorations for the tree. But he also remembers that time as one of the happiest Christmases he ever spent. You made your own fun in those days.

"With things so bad, you'd think Dad would have packed up and gone back to Illinois," said Herman, shaking his head. "Why he didn't I'll never know. Maybe he was just too proud to go back there defeated like that."

It was those tough, droughty days that temporarily turned young Herman into a sheepman. To save their herds, two local sheepmen decided to drive their herds to Suffield, about 150 miles to the northeast where they could get more grazing. Along with each band of sheep went a team and wagon and twelve-year-old Herman was hired to drive one of them. The other was driven by a fourteen-year-old named, Rex Harker, son of one of the owners.

The first night out on the prairie, Herman started to cry and nobody could figure why, not even Herman. Finally, he came to the conclusion he was homesick, never having been away from his folks before. Once he decided what the trouble was, he quit crying, and at the end of the two-month drive, he figured he was a seasoned hand.

But he wasn't such a seasoned hand that he couldn't get lost. It happened when the herds reached the Bow River and had to ferry across, a few at a time. The job took two days.

For some reason, Herman was fascinated by the ferry which he lingered to watch operate long after the herds had moved on. When he set out after the others, he came to a fork in the road just above the river. Which one should he take? Apparently it didn't occur to him that a few thousand sheep would leave marks somewhere on the sod. He swung his wagon onto the right fork, but that didn't lead him anywhere because that track soon forked again. It was long after dark before he found the sheep camp and was able to rejoin his mates.

Eventually better times did come along for the Linders and their neighbors. The family concentrated its efforts on growing feed and raising cattle, which meant they had to get a few horses to work them. But there was seldom any money for extras. For Warner and Herman, the main pleasure was riding horses.

"Of course, we didn't mind that," Herman grinned. "As far as we were concerned, that's what we came out West for anyway."

Although the boys had little chance to see what was going on in the big world outside, that didn't stop them from wondering about it. Around that time, a desperado and his girl friend had shot a policeman in the Crows Nest area and then made for the border via Cardston with the Law hot on their heels. They were caught and promptly hung, which made big news in Cardston for several days.

All this publicity about hanging made Herman and Warner wonder what it was like to be hanged, so they decided to find out. They rigged up a rope over a beam in the old barn and then drew straws to see who would be hung. Warner drew the short one, so he got up on a stool and Herman put the noose around his neck. Then Herman kicked the stool away.

"He was supposed to holler when he'd had enough," said Herman, "but he just hung there without saying a word. After a bit, I got worried and cut him down. He just lay there for a while all quiet and I got real scared. Then he came to and sat up.

" 'Why didn't you holler?' I asked in an aggrieved tone."

"How the hell could I with that rope choking me?" his brother finally bellowed, rubbing the tender spot on his neck.

Another thing they used to wonder about was what it was like to be shot in the rear end with a shotgun loaded

with salt. They were always reading about that happening
to somebody. One day they decided to find out first hand,
so they removed the pellets from some shotgun shells and
stuffed the cartridges with salt. Then they got their father's
shotgun and loaded up. This time, Warner insisted that
Herman be on the receiving end.

"I turned my back and he let me have it from about
300 yards away," said Herman, "but I didn't feel a thing.
Then he tried it from 150 yards and I still didn't feel
anything and I told him all those things we'd heard about
salt-filled shotguns must be wrong.

"Next time, Warner put the muzzle of that old gun just
a few inches from the seat of my pants and pulled the
trigger. Let me tell you when that wad hit I sure felt it! I
jumped a mile but I still didn't let a peep out of me.

" 'That didn't hurt either,' I told him when I had
recovered my balance, 'now let me try it on you.'

"Warner shook his head and grinned. 'Nothing doing,'
he said, 'you jumped too high.' "

But the main amusement for the Linder boys was
riding horses. There used to be a little open range in the
hills west of their place, toward Chief Mountain, and
people would run their horses there in the summertime.

"Our Sunday sport was gathering those horses and
bringing them in," Herman recalled. "We built ourselves a
side-delivery chute and had a little rodeo practically every
Sunday. You might say that's how we got started."

Herman's first actual contact with a bronc came when
he was only twelve years old, and contact is about the best
way to describe it. He had been bugging some cowboys to
let him sit on a bronc and they finally boosted him aboard
a huge horse equipped with an old-fashioned saddle with a
long saddle horn. That saddle horn came in mighty handy,
because before he knew it, that horse took off in a series of
hops that would make a kangaroo turn green with envy.
He found himself hanging on desperately with both
hands.

"I don't think I ever had a horse buck that hard again,"
he laughed. "Those cowboys were just about doubled over

at the sight. They said sometimes I had both my feet straight up in the air. I couldn't walk properly for a month afterwards!"

But those cowboys also noticed something they were to remember long afterwards. Young Herman stayed right with that horse until the critter quit.

Even if Linder senior had moved the family back to Illinois, it's doubtful if the boys would have stayed there very long. Already they were as western as the sage-dotted grasslands that stretched away to the east and south like a great sea. The music of the hoofbeats that had so thrilled their senses that first night in the Cahoon Hotel had become a part of them. They were attuned to the rhythm of the ride, the creak of saddle leather, and the jingle of harness. Horses were as essential to them now as eating and sleeping.

Writing in the magazine *West,* Calgary Stampede founder, Guy Weadick, who was a good friend of the Linders, had this to say of those early years: "Herman and his brother took to riding yearling steers at every opportunity, each trying to outdo the other. It was not long before the yearlings did not offer enough excitement to the young riders. About two years after they started on the calves they were crawling up on full-grown sniffy steers and horses, either bareback, with surcingle or with saddle.

"Herman's brother seemed to be the hard-luck rider of the two. His mounts seemed to fall with him, run into things, or into or over fences that would result in severely bruised or broken bones. They were always pals, and Herman claims that, as a rider, his brother is better than he is. His own success is due, more than anything else, to the help and advice of his brother."

Herman and his brother, Warner, are still inseparable. If one has money the other has it, his closest friends say. And Herman still says Warner could have been one of the "all-time greats" of his day if he hadn't elected to stay on the farm and keep things going.

As Herman recalls, some of those range horses of his

boyhood days would have made good competition saddle broncs.

"Those we did manage to get a saddle on really did buck," he said. "If they had horses like that today some of them would be great rodeo stock."

Warner believes those range strays weren't so very tough to ride. Some of them even had shoes on, but it all added up to a lot of good sport for the Linder boys.

"We had friends from town who liked to come out and visit us, and they always wanted to have a crack at riding these horses," he chuckled. "I never did see kids so scared in my life. They no sooner got on a horse than they jumped off and ran away from him.

"Why Herman and I got so enthused about this cowboy stuff, I don't know," he continued. "I don't see how you can say we had it in us. Our parents weren't ranch people when they came out here. And we sure never dreamt our Sunday afternoon fun would ever turn into a business."

But turn into a business it did and a business that paid more money than they could ever have made on the farm.

Warner did some rodeo riding and roping after Herman began to make it a career, and he won his share of prizes too, as witness a newspaper headline of 1936: "Cardston Brothers Take Premier Prizes." And the story continued: "Staging a brother act in which they held the spotlight through most of the 1936 Calgary Stampede and emerged with many of the final honors between them, Herman and Warner Linder, Cardston cowboys, finished the week of cowboys sports Saturday in a blaze of glory at the top of the aggregate of outstanding Canadian and American rodeo performers."

With their winnings, the brothers were able to help their father get more land and stock, which meant somebody had to stay home and help with the growing work load. Warner decided this was what he really wanted to do.

"I stayed pretty much out at the ranch," he said. "Oh, I went down into the States a little — to Shelby or Great Falls or Browning, Montana, and those places that are fairly close to home. Then I rode at Calgary, Lethbridge, Raymond, and Fort Macleod, and a couple of times at Swift Current, Saskatchewan. And I went to Australia once with Herman."

"Funny thing about that Australia trip," Herman laughed. "I told those fellas down there that Warner didn't ride broncs much — that his long suit was bulldogging steers. Well sir, as it turned out, I beat him in the bulldogging and he took the bronc riding."

When Herman began to hit the rodeo circuit in earnest, he kept his finger in the pie back home by hiring a man to work in his place while he was gone. In between seasons he came right home and pitched in mending fences, hauling feed, and riding herd on the cattle along with the others. All the extra money he could save was used for buying more cattle. He was still very much the farm boy and his thoughts were never very far from the home place and Cardston, nestling below the mountains of the Waterton-Glacier National Parks.

CHAPTER THREE

THE BIGGEST THRILL

"The biggest thrill of my life," said Herman Linder, "was a bright, sunny day at Cardston Rodeo in 1924 when I had my first real competition ride. There I was, with my heart going like a triphammer and my stomach in knots, perched above a real name-bronc in the chutes, just waiting for the announcer to call my turn.

"I wasn't scared, I was just excited. As a matter of fact, at that moment I wouldn't have traded places with the King of England. Here I was, a kid of sixteen, that nobody in rodeo had ever heard of, competing with riders who had established pretty big reputations for themselves.

"Even the horses were better known than I was," he added with a chuckle. "You see, the Cardston rodeo and some of the other small ones held their shows just before the Calgary Stampede. Some of the top riders and horses would stop off there on their way to Calgary and people would come from all over the place just to see these riders and horses.

"So there I was perched up there, sweating a little, but proud as a peacock in the spring. Then suddenly my name was called. I was so excited I just nodded to the gateman and away we went. After that, I was too busy to think of anything but staying on that horse."

That first horse that Herman drew was a reputation bronc named Montana Red and Herman did so well on him and the one that followed he made it right into the finals. That was when the real test came, because this time he drew Yellow Fever, a bronc that was said to be as tough on riders as the pestilence it was named after.

"Just as I was waiting to get on Yellow Fever, a cowboy came by the chute," Herman said. "I don't remember his name, but he was about six-foot-two and he had beautiful spotted chaps and the fanciest hat I ever saw. All I had was a battered old hat and worn cowboy boots and I sure envied him.

"Well, sir, he looked up at me and grinned and said, 'You'll be all right kid, if you just put a little glue in your pants.' And a few of the fellas around there laughed. You know, that didn't sit too well with me and I said to myself, 'Mister, I'll show you'."

And Herman did just that. He rode that horse as if he were out for a joy ride on a roller coaster. When the dust cleared, Yellow Fever had learned that you can't count on a sixteen-year-old kid being a pushover and Herman had come off as the top bronco buster of the show. And Herman learned something too — that it takes more than fancy duds to make a champion. Somehow that gave him a lot of encouragement. He was feeling so proud of himself that he figured he could ride just about anything.

"Well, I wasn't so proud of myself that I decided to march right off and become a professional rodeo rider," Herman hastened to add. "I was still a farm boy at heart and had no plans to do anything else. But fate plays a big part in life and my life was no exception. From then on, events sort of pushed me into rodeo."

About that time, the first Association saddle came out with a fourteen-inch tree — that's the seat you sit on in the saddle — and without the swell which came over the leg of the old "form-fitter" saddle. "If you had a short seat, it was pretty hard to buck you out of the form-fitter saddle once you got down there," Herman explained. "Well, they came out with this new saddle with a fourteen-inch tree and the bulges cut off. In 1925, we got a new saddle from Visalia, California and we had it made with the bulges cut off like the Association saddle, only we had them put a thirteen-inch tree on it. A thirteen-inch tree was fine for one of those form-fitter saddles, but when you had those swells cut off you had to have a longer tree. We didn't learn that lesson until later.

"I suppose the principle is, if somebody throws you a ball and you keep your hands right there, it's going to hurt pretty bad," he continued, "but if you bring your hands back a little the little bit of play in there takes up a lot of the force. The same thing with a saddle. By having that bit of play in the seat you could ride a real rank horse."

But the development of a new type of saddle for bronco busting was only part of it. Herman had to be brought in contact with that saddle so he could learn one of the major rules for success in rodeo: to become a professional, it pays to have professional equipment.

Herman's first ride in a regulation saddle came in 1928, and it all started with a ride in a new car. At that time, E. W. (Ted) Hinman was teaching school in the Cardston area and boarding at the Linders'. Hinman, who later became Provincial Secretary in the Social Credit government of Premier E. C. Manning, had just bought a brand-new Model A Ford equipped with a gear shift and was eager to try it out.

Ted Hinman was also a budding jockey and he decided to drive the fifty miles east to the Raymond Rodeo to give his car a workout — and also to pick up a few dollars riding in the races, if he could. He asked Herman to come along with him and try his hand at bronc riding while he rode in the races.

Herman agreed eagerly. Half the attraction for him was the chance to ride in this beautiful new automobile. It had a gear shift and all kinds of wonderful new gadgets on it. Herman took his California saddle along — the one with the thirteen-inch tree.

In those days they had horse racing, saddle bronc riding and maybe calf roping, or wild cow milking at the smaller rodeos, but no bareback bronc riding competitions. Instead they paid riders what they called "mount money" to ride horses and steers bareback. You generally picked up three dollars for riding one of the horses and one dollar for riding a steer.

Herman won third money in the bronc riding at Raymond and Ted Hinman won a couple of races. Herman even picked up a bit of mount money. More important, they had such a good time doing it they decided to go on to the Milk River rodeo which was being held the day after the Raymond show.

Herman didn't get anywhere in the saddle bronc riding at Milk River. But when it was over, the rodeo people asked if anybody wanted to ride mount money for three dollars. You didn't have to stay on any number of seconds or anything, all you had to do was get on the horse. Even if it bucked you off on the first jump, you got your three dollars.

"Sure, I'll ride one of them," Herman said. "By golly, I'd ride one of those horses all day for three dollars!"

While they were bringing his third horse into the chute for him, the day's bronc riding winner, Joe Fisher, accompanied by Barney Hogg, stopped and asked Herman where he got the saddle he was using.

This was quite a thrill for Herman. Fisher had won third money at Calgary that year and Hogg had made quite a name for himself at several rodeos, so they were "big shots" as far as Herman was concerned. He followed rodeo news just as most kids today follow hockey and football, and could tell you who won what in almost any rodeo in the country. Both these men had been at Raymond, but Herman hadn't spoken to them there because he figured he didn't belong in the company of such heroes. Flattered, he told Fisher he'd ordered the saddle from California.

"Kid," said Fisher, kindly, "that short fork saddle would buck off the best rider in the world. How about letting us put a decent outfit on this next horse. Barney and I figure if you had a decent outfit you'd make one hell of a good bronc rider."

That was the first inkling Herman had that his California made-to-order saddle wasn't the best thing for bronc riding, but he was so thrilled these big-name people had been watching him perform he just nodded gratefully. He had been around rodeos enough to know it wasn't very often a rodeo star did anything to help a young kid just coming into the game.

"You see, son," Fisher told him, "your stirrup leathers are about a quarter inch thick and that makes it hard for you to spur your horse. And your spurs are too long. You should cut them off about half so you can get your foot closer in to the horse's flank."

"And next time you ride, kid," advised Barney Hogg, "you should cut those chaps down. They're like pantaloons. Cut them so they fit tight to your leg, savvy?"

By this time Herman began to feel as if he didn't know anything. But he accepted their advice. In those days, they didn't have rodeo schools for young would-be rodeo riders. Most of the time you had to learn the hard way, which meant looking up from the ground at the heaving saddle you'd been in a moment before and wondering how you got there.

Herman watched while they put one of their saddles on his horse. He noted it had a tree that was a full inch longer than his and it had light latigo fenders. There was even a nice, soft braided rope for a halter shank instead of the hard-twist rope he had used.

Then it was time to mount up. Before he knew it, he was out the gate and jolting across the infield. Never had he experienced such a nice and easy ride: it was like riding a sedan chair. Now he knew how important it was to have the right equipment, especially if he were going to make a career of rodeo.

"Golly!" he exclaimed when he got back to the chutes. "That's the best ride I ever had in my life! How about you fellas selling me that saddle?"

"Not a chance, kid," Fisher told him. "That's a special saddle and we need it in our business."

But Herman kept pestering them about it all afternoon. He wanted that saddle more than anything in the world. More to get rid of him than anything else, Barney Hogg finally agreed he could have it for fifty dollars.

Herman was doubtful as he could buy a new one for forty-five dollars. But Hogg insisted that was the price, thinking that would be the end of it.

When Ted Hinman returned from his race, he found Herman sitting on a corral fence staring thoughtfully off into space.

"How did you make out?" he asked.

"I just had the easiest bronc ride in my life," Herman said. "The horse was a hammer-headed bay, ornery and stubborn as a mule and I just sat there like I was in a parlor coach."

Then Herman told him about the special saddle that Fisher and Hogg had put on for him. Ted asked how much money he had, at which Herman turned out his pockets to reveal about twenty-four dollars. With Ted's contribution, they had fifty-two dollars.

"See, no trouble at all," said Ted."We'd still have two dollars left over. We just filled the gas tank this morning, so we'll have no trouble getting home."

With this saddle, Herman could see the World rodeo crown falling into his lap like a ripe plum. He set off happily with Ted Hinman to find the two riders.

"Tell you what I'll do," he said, when he came up to them. "I'll buy that saddle of yours for fifty dollars, if you'll throw in that halter shank. I'll need that too."

"Well, I'll say this for you," said Fisher, still not too happy about parting with the saddle, "you're a persistent little cuss. Okay, it's a deal."

"If you keep after these broncs like you've kept after us, they're going to find you mighty hard to get rid of," observed Barney Hogg, not realizing this statement qualified him as one of the all-time great prophets.

CHAPTER FOUR

OLD PARDNER

Gathering horses in off the range was fine sport, but Herman and Warner Linder found they had to spend quite a bit of time weeding out the non-buckers. It was too much of a chore to saddle and unsaddle a horse if the animal didn't turn out to be a good bucker.

"We worked out a plan where we'd try each horse first with a mane hold," Herman explained. "If it could buck us off with a mane hold, then we would go to the trouble of putting a saddle on it. But what we were really looking for was a horse that would buck all the time."

The brothers had just about given up on their quest when they ran into a neighbor who told them he had a big black gelding that really knew how to buck. A bit skeptical of this, Herman and Warner went to his place to try out the horse.

The animal proved to be halter broken and seemed quite gentle to handle. Herman tried him first.

"I got alongside of him in a small round corral," he said, "and then I got a good mane hold and in a flash I was on his back. In one jump he flipped me high in the air. I made a complete somersault and landed on my back outside the corral fence, which was only about five feet high."

Warner did ride the animal with their form-fitter saddle, but he could see he was a tough one. "We've got to get this horse," he said to Herman. "I think he's just what we've been looking for!"

"But we haven't got any money," Herman pointed out.

"Maybe we can work a trade on him," his brother said.

When they told their father about their problem, Linder senior looked around to see what they had that was tradeable. There were a few scrub pigs kicking about the place — ten, to be exact. They were theirs if they could work a trade. Maybe their neighbor might like the idea of having a fresh side of pork whenever he fancied it.

The brothers went to their neighbor with the proposition and he was delighted at the prospect.

"What do you call this horse," they asked as they put a halter on him, ready to lead him home.

"We call him old Pardner," the neighbor said, thinking what a good trade he had made.

Herman and Warner didn't know it at the time, but they now had in their possession one of the greatest bucking horses they were ever to encounter.

"Pardner loved to buck!" Herman recalled. "Put a regular form-fitter saddle on him and we could ride him without much trouble. But as soon as we rigged him with that Association saddle with its thirteen-inch tree, it was another story and one that always had the same rough ending. We tried him with that competition saddle every day for two weeks — both of us — and each time we hit the dirt.

"When he bucked us off we would bring him in and give him a feed of oats. He got so that every time he dumped us he'd come running to the corral on his own, looking for that feed. I guess he figured he had done his part and now he wanted his reward."

Herman and Warner soon found that here was one horse they just couldn't master and they began to get pretty discouraged. It seemed if they couldn't ride an old farm horse with regulation equipment they had better forget about ever being rodeo stars. So they gave up all idea of rodeo careers right then and there. They used Pardner to herd cattle and later even put him to work.

"He was a big black horse and gentle as a dog," said Herman, "and he got a little lazy just being used to tend cattle, so we harnessed him and used him for hauling."

Herman left the farm for a while after he and Warner decided they would never make it in rodeo. His sister, Minnie, who was now Mrs. Fred Ingram and living in Cutbank, Montana, wrote to tell him about a job down there.

With three silver dollars clanking in his pocket, nineteen-year-old Herman left for Cutbank with high hopes. It was 1926 and money was scarce, although the real depression hadn't started yet. Much to his disappointment, he didn't get the job, so he hopped on a freight that was headed West, climbing nimbly into an empty box car.

As the train gathered speed, a burly traveller headed for Herman's car at a fast run and Herman helped him to climb aboard. Just then it occurred to him that here he was with three dollars in his pocket and alone with a stranger who might just decide to knock him on the head and take his money.

When the newcomer asked Herman where he was from, Herman said, "I've just been let out of jail". The stranger left the box car hurriedly at the next stop.

Herman jumped off the freight at Spokane where he sampled the hospitality of the U.S. Army for about three weeks before deciding he didn't want to be a soldier. Then he ran into a man wo told him he could get him a job on a Great Northern Railway construction crew for seventy-five dollars a month. Herman worked at that job all winter and then returned home in time for seeding — back to his family and old Pardner and the big career that awaited both of them a few years down the road.

The brothers had a lot of fun with Pardner. When a young Mountie friend in Cardston who had done a little riding at one time heard they had acquired a pretty good bucking horse, he asked if he could come and have a try at him some day. Herman and Warner arranged that he come out the next Sunday. They passed the word around to their friends and come Sunday quite a crowd had assembled at the farm.

When the policeman arrived, the horses were all waiting in the corral.

"Which one is Pardner?" he wanted to know.

Herman pointed to a bald-faced bay horse over in one corner.

"Say, that is a U-necked, ornery-looking critter!" the Mountie nodded. "Maybe I'd better not tackle him right off the bat. Have you got anything else around that might buck a little bit?"

Warner nodded and pointed to the real Pardner, who was gazing with a sort of mild interest at the goings-on. "That black one over there may buck a little," he said, "providing you spur him hard enough."

The brothers had Pardner rigged with a surcingle and they ran him into the chute so the policeman could get on.

"I haven't been riding for quite a while," the Mountie reminded them.

"That's all right," Herman said. "That horse has a surcingle with two hand holds on it. If you haven't been riding for some time maybe for this first ride you'd better use both hands."

"Remember to spur him hard," Warner advised. "You really have to spur him high up on the neck or he won't buck at all. After all, we don't want to disappoint the crowd of people who came out here to watch."

Pardner came out of that chute like a runaway express train! He took two great jumps and that Mountie went flying through the air as if he were shot out of a cannon. As he came limping back, knocking the dust from his clothes, the policeman shook his head. "If that old horse you say can't buck worth a hoot can toss me so easy, what in hell must that Pardner be like!"

That spring, some young fellas came out from town and said they'd like a chance to ride. One of them, named

Faye Smith, who was almost six feet tall and about seventeen years old, was particularly anxious to get on a real bucker. He didn't want to waste his time on any old plow horse, or anything like that.

"Maybe Pardner there can buck a little," Herman nodded.

When they saw those long legs on the kid, they tried to let the stirrups out to give him all the break they could. But their guest wanted to double his feet up like he'd seen jockeys do in the movies.

"No, no, that's no good," Herman told him, "you won't have a prayer if you try to ride him that way."

Young Smith allowed them to let out the stirrups as they suggested, but even that didn't help him much. Old Pardner came charging out, gave a couple of quick leaps, and the kid went flying through the air. He went off home nursing his tailbone. But next day he was back, determined to have his way this time.

"Where's old Pardner?" he asked.

"Out there in the field," Warner pointed.

"Well," said the kid, eyeing them slyly, "I'd like to try him again."

Smith really thought the Linders were trying to fix him with this long stirrup business. He knew the right way to ride a horse was with your knees up high, like he'd seen real race jockeys do. There was no way they could convince him to get his feet down.

The brothers had just scraped the manure out of the corral and a big, soft pile of it lay out on the field a short distance from the chute.

Pardner's method was always to come out of the chute at a run before exploding into action. He would turn to the left, take a few violent jumps, swing left again, then take a few more jumps that jarred you all the way up your spine. If you were still there after that, he'd keep on turning and jumping until you felt like you'd been spun around like a top.

But young Smith was not so durable. Pardner made his run and when he suddenly busted in two, he was right beside this big dung pile. There was that qick shift to the left and the kid shot into the pile of manure with his hands held high.

"Whew — Shit!" he exclaimed disgustedly as he crawled out of it. That was the last time he ever tried to ride Pardner, legs up or down.

Pardner's reputation spread slowly, but surely, around the district. But it was to be a couple of years before he was used in a real rodeo. Then, for some reason the newspapers started calling the horse, Pardner Brown.

At that time, Ray Knight was stock contracting bucking horses for the Cardston Rodeo. He had lots of horses, but he was always ready to take a look at one with special bucking talents.

"What will you give me if I bring a real good bucking horse to your rodeo?" Warner asked him. "I'll bring you one that will buck off anybody who comes to the competition, say for five dollars? If anybody can stay on him you don't have to pay me anything," Warner added.

"Okay," Ray nodded. "If you can bring me a horse like that you'll get your five dollars."

Herman drove the farm pickup while Warner rode Pardner the six miles into town. As Herman drove into the rodeo grounds, Ray Knight came over to see him.

"Say, where's that bucking horse you were going to bring?" Knight asked.

"Right here," said Warner, who had just ridden up behind them. He dismounted, took the saddle off Pardner, and tossed it in the back of Herman's truck.

Ray Knight looked a little bewildered but he didn't say anything. A former bronc buster himself, he was a regular old-timer around the rodeo circuit, so he figured anything was possible. What bothered him was the idea of anybody riding to the show on what was supposed to be an "untamed outlaw". It made their advertising look a bit foolish. Herman and Warner knew what was going through the stock contractor's head, but they just grinned and turned old Pardner loose with the other horses.

The first day, the rider that drew Pardner didn't have much experience and the horse bucked him off just about as soon as they left the chutes. The second day was the same. Maybe Pardner was getting a little mad that he was doing all this work and not getting his usual feed of oats. That should have been the end of it, because even then the rules said that a horse was not to be used twice in the same contest by different contestants.

But Slim Watrin was at this rodeo. Slim had won at the Calgary Stampede and was one of the top bronco busters in the rodeo world at that time. He had drawn a real dog on the last day and needed a reride which would give him lots of points.

Ray Knight was beginning to have a lot of respect for Pardner. Nevertheless, he was sure Slim Watrin wouldn't have any trouble with this farm horse, and if Slim rode Pardner, Knight wouldn't have to pay the five bucks. After all, that's what Warner Linder had agreed. Knight went down and tossed a rope on Pardner and brought him to the chutes.

"Slim was terribly hard to bring down," Warner recalled. "He was what we called a one-legged rider. That is, he spurred like hell with one foot and kept the other anchored in the stirrup."

Pardner came charging out like he always did, then he started his swings and hops. But Watrin was staying right with him. After about seven seconds, the horse busted loose with all he had and Slim sailed ten feet into the air.

"Pardner was still coming around in a circle when Slim hit the ground," chuckled Warner. "He was a neck-reined saddle horse. If a right-handed guy rode him, he went right — if the rider was left-handed, he went left. Then Pardner went over to Slim and sniffed at him, probably looking for his oats.

"Well, sir, I just yelled at him and he came to me. Then I swung into the saddle and rode him up and down in front of the stands. The crowd went wild. I guess Slim Watrin never forgave me for that. Ray Knight wasn't very happy about it either."

"You should have seen his face," Herman chuckled. "It looked like a thundercloud over Chief Mountain. He said things like that ruined the image of rodeo. How was he going to convince anybody they used nothing but wild, unbroken horses after that?

"And the nice thing about it was that Pardner was so gentle," Herman added. "Warner even used to take his girl friend out riding on him. Warner would sit at the back and she would sit in the saddle and they'd go off riding down the road together. It's hard to believe that horse was a real bucker."

After his first season in professional rodeo, Herman returned to the ranch and invested his winnings in cattle. The next day he and Warner were out looking the place over and Herman caught sight of Pardner in the corral, half snoozing in the warm sunshine.

"You know," said Herman to his brother. "I wonder if that old galoot is really as good as we used to think he was? I've been riding some pretty rank horses on the circuit the past year. I just wonder if old Pardner can still buck me off."

Without another word, they took the big gelding into the field. Pardner was not overawed by Herman who had so recently won the Canadian championship. In Herman's own words, Pardner threw him "higher than a woodpecker's nest".

CHAPTER FIVE

CARDSTON TO CALGARY

In 1929, the year following Herman's first official rodeo ride, he was using his precious Association saddle to break horses for a rancher south of the line in Montana. "They were a pretty rough string of horses," Herman said. "The trouble was their owner had started trying to break them, but the horses had gotten the best of him. By the time he decided to give me and some other fellas a chance at them, the animals were a lot harder to handle because they'd been spoiled. You see, it's much easier to break a horse if you've had him right from the start.

"No matter how we tried to keep them from bucking, every once in a while one of them would break in two and really start acting up. But none of them ever did actually buck me off all the time I was over there, though maybe they had me grabbing leather a couple of times."

One of the men on the horse-breaking crew with Herman was a rider named Gordon DeBray, who had placed third in the roping at Calgary one year and could really handle the manila. When they had finished breaking the American broncs, DeBray made a suggestion that was to catapult Herman into the career he had been drifting toward all the time.

"Let's you and me take a couple of weeks holiday and go to the Calgary Stampede," he said, "and on our way maybe we can stop at the Sweetgrass Rodeo and try our luck."

Herman agreed. And just to prove what a good idea it was, he picked up $100 in the bronc riding at that small Montana town next day. The financial world may have been ready to crash about them, but Linder had already turned the corner that would lead to prosperity. It would have taken a lot of hard work and penny pinching to save $100 on the farm.

He and his friend headed north in fine spirits. When they got to High River, they decided to try their luck again. The High River rodeo was held on a Friday and Saturday just before the Monday opening of the Calgary Stampede. And it was no amateur contest as they soon found out when they got to the rodeo grounds on the northwest edge of town. A lot of the big name riders were there to give themselves a bit of a workout before the big show.

"Golly, I don't know," Herman said to DeBray as he read the formidable list of contestants. "I have an idea I'd just be wasting my entry fee here."

On the list were Dan Utledge from Texas and Earl Thode, the outstanding bronco buster from Casa Grande, Arizona, a former World Champion bronc rider and one of the best ever to come out of the United States. On down the list, Herman could see the names of top-flight Canadian champions: there were the famous Watrin brothers, Joe Fisher, who had sold him his highly-prized Association saddle, and Smoky Snyder. Next, was the boy who was to become known as the greatest bronc rider of them all, Pete Knight.

"It was the first time I'd ever seen Pete Knight, the Watrin boys, George McIntosh, and Frank Sharp," Herman recalled, "not to mention Harry Knight and Lee Ferris, Canada Kid. Most of these fellows were in the habit of winning world championships as regularly as a cow bloats on fresh alfalfa."

Even against this tough competition, Herman won first day money and third day money in the bareback bronc riding and one first in saddle bronc day money. But as far as he was concerned, rodeo was still just a holiday break away from his regular work.

"What with the money I had won at Sweetgrass and my High River money, I already had enough to pay for my holiday," he said. "I was a pretty happy cowboy, let me tell you. But there was still no thought of making rodeo my career. As far as everybody at that show was concerned, I was just a kid from Cardston who liked to ride. And that's how I thought of myself. I was having the time of my life hobnobbing with all these rodeo greats."

Though he didn't know it, Herman's victory parade had already begun. As they headed up to the big show on the weekend, his friend Gordon remarked that they might as well enter in some of the events. If nothing else, it would give them the right to sit in the competitors stand where they could get a good close look at all the infield events. Herman agreed.

The result was blazoned across the front pages of the Calgary newspapers of that day. When the dust had settled on the final go round the "Kid from Cardston" was a champion twice over. He had won the Canadian Bronc Riding Championship with Saddle and also the Canadian Bareback Bronc Riding Championship. To add to the "loot" won in the two smaller shows, he had over $1,000 in cash and two gold watches. Runner-up in the competition was the famous Pete Knight.

Herman still looks back almost in disbelief on that chain of fast-moving events that catapulted him into the limelight.

"In those days, they had two Saddle Bronc competitions, one the Canadian Saddle and one they called the North American Saddle," he explained. "The Canadian was open to everybody, so it wasn't an amateur event. It decided the championship of Canada and the North American was open to anybody in the world. I was entered in both competitions and with every horse I rode in the day monies I was placing — I was placing right along. I was also in the Canadian Bareback event. No sense just sitting around watching, I figured.

"What you did in those days," he continued, "was you rode two horses the first four days, then everybody who had qualified would ride another horse in what they called the semi-finals on Friday. Those who qualified on Friday got to ride another horse on Saturday for the finals. It was a four horse average. Anyway, I was in both the North American and the Canadian Saddle events. I didn't finish in the final money in the North American, but I did win the Canadian Saddle and Bareback Championships. That was quite a thrill for me, to think a twenty-two-year-old novice could beat a man like Pete Knight!

"You see, I had really lost three years of the best riding time of my life — from 1925 to 1928 — because I didn't know anything about proper rodeo equipment," he said. "Strange as it may seem, that's how little I knew about rodeo. Even in the finals, I thought to myself, that's fine, I've won myself some good money during this week. I never dreamt about placing first in the final money and winning two championships!

"When I looked at the program and saw the amount of money I had won, it was like a dream. There was $500 and a gold watch for the Saddle Bronc Championship and $300 and another gold watch for the Bareback Championship. That $800 was more money than I had ever hoped to see in my life all at one time. And then the day money added to this made it well over $1,000.

"One of my greatest thrills was that Saturday night when they awarded the prizes over at the grandstand. There I was, standing with a gold watch in each hand with the fireworks exploding all around me. The thought that I still had $800 cash money to collect over at the office was almost too much for me. Of course I was to see many such days after that, but they never did seem quite the same."

By now, Herman was beginning to believe he was really cut out to be a professional rodeo rider. He never did go back to breaking horses on the range, but sent back word to the Montana rancher he was working for that he

figured he could make more money at the rodeo game —
which turned out to be the understatement of the year — if
not the century. In the Depression you could break your
backside a thousand times over before you ever made
$1000 breaking horses.

Said Guy Weadick, who produced that Stampede
show of 1929: "For the next ten years Herman was
destined to ride the ripples of that first big splash."

For the rest of that first season, Herman palled around
with Lee Ferris, Canada Kid, who was from DeWinton,
just south of Calgary. And he learned a lot from Ferris.
Guy Weadick figured the Kid had no equal when it came
to courage and stamina. When one year a Brahma bull the
Kid was riding at the Calgary Stampede hooked out his
left eye, he was taken to a doctor right away and the doctor
removed the injured optic. Two days later, the Kid was
back at the rodeo grounds demanding the remainder of his
rides.

But, in Linder's opinion, the best man for any young
rider to pattern himself after was Pete Knight.

"Pete used to sit well in the saddle, with just enough
rein," he said, "and he would kick the horse high in the
neck as soon as it started to buck. He was the best rider I
ever saw because he rode steadier on harder horses than
anybody else. There were quite a few who spurred as
much or more than Pete, but they generally got bucked off
the tougher horses."

After his big win at his first Calgary show, Herman
went to Vancouver, B.C. where he picked up another $200
in day money. The following year, he appeared at many of
the smaller Canadian rodeos, entering in all events on the
program. But drawing him like a magnet was the Calgary
Stampede where he was destined to become the Canadian
All Around Cowboy Champion seven times, and the
North American All Around Champion five times.

In his book *Calgary Stampede*, veteran newspaperman
and rodeo authority, Fred Kennedy, named Linder as one
of the small band of spectacular performers who returned
to Calgary year after year to add to their laurels. Said

Kennedy, "In this rare category were men like Herman Linder of Cardston, Alberta, a slim-waisted young cowboy who appeared on the rodeo scene in the late twenties and who, in less than eight years of competition, amassed the staggering total of twenty-two championship titles. Strangely enough, Linder never won a world championship, but he dominated the Canadian scene for years, in addition to winning many State championships. One of the reasons for his failure to win a world title was simply that he competed in too many events. He won championships in bronc riding contests with saddle, bareback bronc riding, wild steer riding, Brahma bull riding and calf roping."

A few years after Herman's first big splash at Calgary, a headline in the *Calgary Herald* announced: "Herman Linder Leading in both Stampede Bronc Riding Contests." And the story went on to say: "Herman Linder, Cardston cowboy, stamped himself as outstanding favorite to win either the Open or the Canadian Bronc Riding crown when he captured first money in the Canadian contest at the Calgary Stampede Tuesday afternoon. Linder had previously placed first in the North American contest on Monday, and, as a consequence, he is leading more than 150 contestants in points to date. Hard kicking bucking horses and salty steers made the cowboys lives miserable all afternoon. Many a bruised and battered cowpoke hauled himself to a nice, quiet spot behind the chutes to rub his bruises and meditate upon the many things that can happen to a cowboy in a championship contest."

Sometimes Herman's ten-year victory sweep had an element of luck to it, as he readily admits. In fact, one Calgary newspaper title read: "Lucky Linder." And the story continued: "Linder's win in the Canadian contest had an element of luck to it. His first horse, Miss Meeks, didn't fire, so he asked for a re-ride. Jack Dillon dived into the hat and out came Black Cat. The saddle was set and Linder climbed aboard. He hit the outlaw once in the shoulders and then came the hurricane! On the third jump, he was higher in the saddle than a Chinese kite in a storm. But he managed to kick himself back. On the fifth jump, the outlaw sunfished and the Cardston cowboy again showed daylight as he scratched frantically to stay aboard. The whistle blew on the ninth jump, and before the echo of the whistle had died away, Linder was bucked clean off the starboard side."

But Calgary continued to be Linder territory for the greater part of Herman's riding career. And his brother, Warner, had a share in making it so. In one contest, Warner shaved more than a second from the World Steer Decorating record when he hung the ribbon on the horn of a plunging steer in three seconds flat. Herman took second place with five and a half seconds. The brothers won no less than four first monies between them in various events.

Seven years after his first Stampede triumph, Herman again cinched his title as All Around North American cowboy for another year by coming out at or near the top spot in every event in which he took part. On the day of the semi-finals, headlines proclaimed: "Friday was Linder Day at the Stampede," and this was due in part to a badly-injured Warner Linder's magnificent efforts in the steer decorating line.

Said the story: "Half crippled with muscles torn from his back, and a broken collar bone, Warner Linder, top steer decorator for this year's event, defied doctor's orders to tackle one of the big, difficult steers Friday. His injuries did not seem to have any effect on the big boy from Cardston for he made his flying tackle with the same skill as on the two previous days and the surprised steer had a little red flag waving from his left horn in 6-2/5 seconds from the time the elder Linder took after him. This makes it three straight for Warner, his two previous times having been 6-2/5 seconds and 6-1/5 seconds, which put him far ahead of the field for this event and he may have set a World record for consecutive decorating."

A year earlier, a headline had proclaimed: "Linder, Pete Knight Share Spotlight," and the story went on to say that "the veteran and tyro rodeo riders celebrated the opening of Calgary Stampede with a wild orgy of spectacular rides at Victoria Park on Monday afternoon."

Herman, who had won more awards at the Calgary Stampede than any other Canadian, was finally honored by having his picture hung in the Calgary Horseman's Hall of Fame.

CHAPTER SIX

HITTING THE ROAD

A rodeo rider builds his reputation by hitting the road and riding the rodeo circuit in the towns and cities of Canada and the United States. After you have been roughly introduced to a few hundred plunging broncs, all the way from the railway whistle stops to the crowded cities, you can call yourself a rodeo cowboy, providing you have the natural talent and your neck isn't broken in the meantime.

Herman generally stayed working around the ranch until June, when the Cardston Rodeo started. Then he rode in the smaller shows close to home, such as Fort Macleod, Lethbridge, Medicine Hat, Raymond, High River, and Browning, Montana, until the Calgary Stampede, which is held in the early part of July.

"After Calgary, we'd usually go to Cheyenne, Wyoming, then Great Falls and Butte, in Montana, and end up away back East sometime in November," said Herman.

Like most young riders just starting out, Herman found those early years on the American circuit a very frustrating business. In many cases, the judges were local bigwigs who knew nothing about rodeo. They generally awarded the prizes to riders they knew, or had heard about. A newcomer didn't have a chance, no matter how well he rode.

"It wasn't like it is now," said Herman. "In those early days, the rodeo rider was just a working stiff. The man who put on the show was the boss, and never let you forget it. You could tell that by the way they talked to you. I remember in 1931 in Chicago. Colonel Johnson who ran the stock there came up to the chutes where a rider was having a job trying to get on his horse. The horse was practically upside down most of the time and the rider was waiting for a chance to drop into the saddle. 'Get on there and ride him!' Johnson yelled at the rider. 'Are you scared of him?'

"That was the way they talked to you. No matter that you weren't even on their payroll, that you had to pay them an entry fee, and then win before you got any money. In many cases, you paid out more than you took in. Some promoters were worse than that — they even skipped out of town before you could collect your prize money!"

What bothered Herman more than anything else was the lack of proper rules and standards for judging. Sometimes a bit of local politics entered into it and you could help your cause along by having a few drinks with the judges. Things didn't change for the better until the riders organized and got the shows to use former competitors as judges.

"Sometimes you ran into that in Canada too," said Herman, "but it was really bad in the States. You'd go to some rodeo where the fella who marked the score was some local store manager who liked to ride around with a big hat and a pair of shiny cowboy boots. He was a member of all the right clubs in town so they made a judge out of him and he didn't know anything. If things had been managed then as they are now, I'd have won in a lot of these places, but I was making some good rides and not getting anywhere."

Cheyenne, Wyoming, was one of the towns where the cards were pretty well stacked against the newcomer, Herman found. There were three or four favorites who rode there. If they rode, you didn't have a chance, no matter how well you did, he remembers.

"In fact, in Cheyenne," he said, "a guy named Burel Mulkey and I should have won first and second place money almost every day. I don't think we ever drew horses that bucked so well. But Burel never even placed one penny, and I didn't do much better. Then third time around I drew a horse that had never been ridden down in that country. The judge came up to me and said, 'Well, good luck to you, kid.' When I got going, I spurred that horse just like the rest of them and I won third money in the finals. You know, that got the officials looking at me just a little bit, as if they had an idea maybe I could ride. But I wouldn't have won if one of the guys that usually won hadn't lost a stirrup and been disqualified.

"The next day," Herman continued, "Earl Thode who had won the Saddle Bronc riding, stopped to talk to me. He was really a nice guy and one of the top riders in the world in his time. He was lugging the saddle he had won and said: 'See this saddle I won. Look at all that fancy silver on it.' And he laughed, 'If they had known you as well as they know me, you would've probably had it.' "

One of the top rodeos in the United States is held at Sidney, Iowa. Although a relatively small town, Sidney has a big rodeo each year put on by the American Legion Post No. 128. It draws huge crowds from all over the state and most of the nation's top riders.

Herman first entered the Sidney Rodeo in 1933, winning the Bull Riding championship and $186. In the next five years, he won three All Around titles and four more event championships. But at first, Herman thought he was going to have the same trouble getting anybody to notice him as he'd had at Cheyenne.

"As it turned out, Sidney proved to be a lucky place for me," he recalled. "I was on my way to Chicago to ride at the World's Fair and stopped off there because I was told they had a big rodeo. Well sir, I rode every saddle bronc, bareback horse, and bull they gave me and I think I should have won on some of them, but I hadn't won a penny. Then I had one more bull to ride on the last night and I knew it had to be a good one. I had only about five dollars left.

"In those days you never knew what animal you drew because the draw was held in secret. Well, there was one bull in there that had never been ridden and I said, 'I sure wish that bull would be in my stall tonight'. And you know, by golly it was! That's the only time in my life a judge ever handed me the book and said, 'Here, you can mark yourself!' He was only joshing of course.

"Well, I rode him and won the day money and average for that event, which was $186. That's why I say after that Sidney always seemed a lucky place for me."

From his victory in Sidney, Herman began what he describes as his "Trek across the Continent". Almost before he realized it, he was in Chicago and in the midst of what Ed Sullivan would call a "really big shew".

"Day money in that show meant something and I pulled into the winnings to the tune of $200 to $400," said Herman. "You talk about there being a Depression on! I never saw any there! Everybody was out to see the rodeo!"

Back home, local papers made a big thing of Herman and other Canadian riders competing at the World's Fair, as witness this headline: "Cardston Rodeo Hero Invited to World's Fair." Said the story: "To be one of thirty contestants in all the World to be invited to participate in the World's Fair Rodeo is some distinction most any cowboy would covet. This distinction came to Herman Linder on Thursday last week, when a direct invitation was received by him to be one of the participants of the rodeo to be held in Soldier's Field in Chicago from August 25th to September 10th. Only thirty contestants in each event are permitted — fifteen in the afternoon show and another fifteen in the evening performance. There are three from all Canada invited to this event". The other two were Pete Knight and Harry Knight.

From Chicago, Herman went on to Boston to new triumphs. It was the first of many Wild West shows to be staged in that city and the Boston papers took special note

of Herman. Said a report in one of the leading dailies:
"The contest last night raised the hair of the spectators
straighter than any of those since the opening night.
Herman Linder of Cardston, Alberta, Canada, made a
clean sweep of the Bareback Bronc Riding event when he
scratched Broomtail into first day money. Canada Kid of
Calgary, Canada, did the required eight seconds aboard
Dillon Bay for second money, while Pete Grubb of
Blackfoot, Idaho, was victor over Burney for third
place."

Proclaimed a headline in another paper: "Herman
Linder of Cardston Alberta Sees the World." And the
story went on to say: "Hobnobbing with the elite of
Boston, who for the first time in their lives saw a real, live
rodeo in the sedate old city of Boston, Herman Linder with
his fellow cowboys from the Great West met in these
famous Boston Gardens and enjoyed a real chuckwagon
meal. Eating in the open with their city friends, all decked
out in ten gallon hats and overalls and the rest of the Wild
West regalia."

"It was such a tremendous success that we were feted
right in the heart of town," was how the young Herman
described it in a newspaper interview, "and the big bugs
dressed up with us along with big hats and overalls and
squatted down to a chuckwagon meal just like common
folks. Tickets sold for one dollar to five dollars a seat and
there were 18,000 people there the first day of the
show."

These were only the first of many headlines Herman
was fated to make in Boston during the ten years of his
active riding career.

The "Kid from Cardston" was very impressed by what
he saw on those early trips around the rodeo circuit. And
he wasn't behind the bush when it came to letting people
know how he felt about all these new experiences.

"New York also attracted me," he said in another
interview, "and we showed in New York with the same
success. But I didn't like the shows they took us to in New
York City. They're all crazy about wrestling there and

they took us to the Garden that night and we saw one big bully mauling another. He would knock his wind out of him and then sit on him. Professional wrestling to me is the poorest sport in the world. A ringside seat in Madison Square Garden isn't worth taking, even when they hand it to you."

Then he goes on to describe a visit to a rope factory: "While in the East, we were taken to the Plymouth Rope factory and, oh boy, they gave us two of the finest hard twist lariats you ever saw each! And they treated us like we were kings. In fact, the East is the most hospitable place in the World to my way of thinking! They certainly do not spare any trouble when they want to show you a good time.

"And the country is lovely!" he continued. "Even in November the trees were still out in leaf and the flowers were showing in New York. And when we left Wyoming and Montana in October, the whole country was a desert!"

Then he apparently thought over what he had just said and maybe felt he was being a little disloyal to the West for he added: "When I think of all the places I have been, though, there aren't many places like Cardston. We even went to see the place where the Pilgrims landed at Plymouth Rock. And if they had ever seen Cardston in their dreams they would never have stayed in that country!"

Then his interviewer asked him if he intended to keep following the rodeo trail after the success he'd had in his first year. And Herman was as definite about that as he was about quitting rodeo when he figured he'd made enought to settle down back home.

"Well yes, I guess I'll go again next year and maybe the next year too, if prices on farm products don't come up," he said. "I can help Dad out on the farm more by bringing home some of that day money than by tending pigs at two cents a pound.

"But I'm going to always come back home," he concluded. "In the spring I expect to do the seeding as usual and stay for the spring work, perhaps even haying, before I set out again in the rodeo business. But I'd rather stay home and I'm going to leave it off just as soon as I can, only perhaps to take in the Calgary Stampede and a few of the shows close in."

This interview shows the clear thinking, the ability to set a goal far ahead, and stay on course until it is reached that has characterized Herman's career from that first "big splash" at the Calgary Stampede in 1929 to the present day. It also shows that natural enthusiasm for all he sees and does which is still so much a part of his personality, in spite of his World travels, the many speaking engagements and the large events of which he has been a part.

Herman may not have cared for the wrestling he saw at New York on that first visit, but he was to become famous in Madison Square Garden for his own particular brand of wrestling as the following excerpts from some of the papers of those early days will show.

From a New York paper: "At the afternoon show, Herman Linder of Cardston dug his gaunt knees into the sides of a crawfishing bay called Old Man of the Mountain and he stuck there as though he was glued. He won that chapter of the bareback contest without so much as losing his sombrero."

And from another: "Herman Linder is one of the attractions of any rodeo. Cowboys and cowgirls at the Gardens here, as also throughout the rodeo circuit, always give their fullest attention when Linder's name is called. Given a good bucking horse, he demonstrates the highest technique of a champion. His spurs rake fore and aft with the precision of a bicycle rider. The arm never gets below his waist and never, of course, touches the horse. Daylight never gets between him and the saddle. He keeps his balance without leaning too far in any way. Scores of cowboys who now rank as good money riders learned their tricks from Linder."

CHAPTER SEVEN

HERMAN GETS THROWED

There's an old range saying that "there's never a hawss that can't be rode and there's never a rider that can't be throwed" and this could be applied to Herman Linder's often-voiced determination to stay single.

"I don't intend to get married as long as I'm on the road," he used to say to anyone who would listen. "It's a tough life and a fella can do much better if he's on his own."

That was before a dark-haired school teacher from Eureka, South Dakota, named Agnes Zeller, came up to Cardston to visit her sister, Mrs. George Wolff. When Herman called at his neighbors, the Wolffs, one evening for a visit, he knew he was about to hit the tanbark harder than any time he had been tossed in the rodeo arena.

They were married in Eureka on Christmas Day, 1932, and next year Agnes found herself travelling on the rodeo circuit with Herman and playing penny ante poker with other rodeo wives in a score of cities that had been only names in the paper to her a short while before.

Although born and raised on a farm outside Eureka, Agnes Zeller had never even ridden a horse, let alone a bronc. In fact, she wasn't to know the feel of saddle leather until some years later when Herman took her to visit a dude ranch near Livingston, Montana.

"As far as I was concerned, one rider in the family was enough," she smiled, "and I was quite content for Herman to have that honor."

Like other rodeo wives, she did a lot of agonizing when her husband was in the arena but she didn't raise any objections to Herman's chosen career. It was what he wanted to do and she was content to go along with him until he himself decided to call it quits.

"It was an entirely new experience for me," she recalled. "We wives always watched when our husbands were riding. In the small towns we used to watch the whole show. Then in the evenings when it was all over someone could be counted on to start a poker game. The men had their games and we had ours."

But when they got to a big city like New York where the rodeo might be on two or three weeks, everybody was too busy to play poker at nights. There was too much to do and see in New York. When Herman wasn't riding, Agnes Linder was always at a show or just walking around looking at the stores.

The first year when Mrs. Linder hit the road with Herman was a memorable year in more ways than one. They set out from Cardston at the end of July in a 1929 Model A Ford with their luggage piled high in the back, including all their heavy winter clothing because they knew they wouldn't be back until November or December.

By the time they reached Chicago, the car was beginning to feel the effects of a few thousand miles of gravel roads and dust clouds. When Herman turned down into the Loop, the engine conked out like a dead mackerel. As the starter wasn't working properly, he had to jump out and crank the engine into life. This happened several times as they progressed through town on their way to Soldier's Field.

After Chicago, they managed to make it as far as St. Louis, when the engine began to sound like it was going to come to pieces. Herman stopped and had a look at it. He found that everything was being shaken loose by the vibration. Another rider from Calgary, George McIntosh, who was travelling with them, helped Herman get things tightened up again.

"One thing sure, this car isn't going to take us to New York and then all the way back home again," said Herman. "We're going to have to get a new one someplace."

Knowing they would have a hard time getting an American car back over the border, they headed north for Windsor, Ontario. There, Linder tried to make a deal for a secondhand car that would at least get them safely home again. The trouble was the dealer didn't have the kind of car Herman needed for the kind of money he could afford. He was too scared to buy a new one at so much a month. You didn't do things like that in the Depression because you never knew if you were going to have the money.

"Tell you what," said George McIntosh, "I've got a sister in Guelph. Maybe her husband can get us a good deal on a car. It always helps when you know somebody."

This turned out to be sound advice. George's brother-in-law took them down to a local garage and there sat a shiny 1931 Model A with only 2,000 miles on its speedometer. It looked like new, it ran like new, and the price was only $200, plus their old car. The Linders were thrilled. This was much better than they had ever hoped for.

"I still had fifty dollars left," Herman recalled with a smile, "and that was enough to get us to the next rodeo, which was at Cleveland, Ohio."

And his luck held. He won first day money in the bronco riding, which helped to shore up his sagging finances.

"The trouble was there were very few people coming to the show," said Herman. "About the middle of the week, the fellow who was promoting the show — his name was Fred Beebe — skiddooed overnight, leaving everybody holding the sack. The rodeo stock had been rented from California and we were all left sitting high and dry. But I still had that first day money, which was fifty dollars, so we were right back where we had been when we left Ontario."

Without a care in the world, the Linders hit out for Washington, D.C. to see the sights before heading up to New York for the big show. When they arrived in New York, they had only ten dollars left.

Herman will never forget that first trip to the metropolis as a married man. "We landed in the big city in the evening," he chuckled, "and we started looking around for an apartment as close to Madison Square Garden as we could get. Finally we found one and we figured our troubles were over. It had a nice big room with a fancy carpet, a floor lamp, and an almost new studio couch that could be made into a bed. There was also a little kitchenette — even a bath tub. But you had to share a toilet down the hall with everybody else. The price was reasonable too.

" 'That'll be ten dollars for the week,' said the landlord, eyeing me carefully, 'in advance.'

" 'Tell you what we'll do,' I told him. 'We're here for the rodeo and we're sure to win some money. As soon as the show's over we'll pay you.'

" 'In advance,' he repeated firmly.

"But I wasn't ready to give up on him yet," Herman grinned. "Ten dollars was all we had and we'd need some money for food, so I decided to play a little bluff poker with him. I thought, gosh, this is the Depression and these guys must want to rent these places pretty badly, so I picked up the suitcases as though I was going to leave. But I soon saw this guy wasn't going to budge an inch, and I set them down again.

"Of course I wasn't going to leave, even if I'd had to pay him the whole ten dollars. But Agnes didn't know what I was thinking. I could see the tears starting down her cheeks. She was tired and didn't want to tramp around looking at suites any more, so I decided I had to do something fast. I offered him five dollars, and to our relief, he took it."

"It's funny looking back on it," his wife admitted, "but all I remember I was dead tired and beginning to think this rodeo business was not as glamorous as I thought it would be. But then we went down to the corner grocery store and got enough stuff to last us for a week. Across from it was the biggest meat market I had ever seen in my whole life. It must have been about a block long. After we got through in there we only had a few cents left of our five dollars. But we came back to the room and put the food in the ice box and I made us the biggest dinner we'd had in a long while."

"One thing I can't figure out," mused Herman, "is how well we slept that night on the makedown bed. Here I hadn't even entered the rodeo yet. I didn't have enough money for the entry fee, but I never slept better in my life! If something like that happened today, I think I'd go crazy with worry."

Herman had no cause to worry. After borrowing the entry fee from another rider, he did some of the best riding of his career. When the show ended, he was crowned King of the Rodeo and shared $4,200 in prize money with six other riders. Being the champion, Herman got the lion's share of the money. He was also presented with a beautiful silver embossed saddle by Madison Square Garden president, Colonel John R. Kilpatrick.

"That seemed to be the turning point for us financially," he recalled, "for from then on we always had money. Yes sir, my luck sure did change for the better when I got married!"

"I loved being in New York," Mrs. Linder said. "I was raised on a Dakota farm, you see, and had never been in a big city before. I wanted to go everywhere and take it all in! After that, I was there every year until Herman quit rodeo."

There was only one fly in the ointment that year, as far as Herman was concerned — a government fly. When he crossed the border bound for home, the Canada Customs officials charged him forty percent duty on his prize saddle. Herman admits he felt pretty sick about that and he still figures those Custom boys were a little rough on him. After all, he was the winner in what is considered the World Series of the rodeo game and he had brought this title to Canada. He thought this country should have taken a little pride in his achievements too.

The press was now calling Herman the continent's greatest rough rider. And the rodeo moguls were billing him as the world's number one all-around cowboy.

Throughout his colorful riding career Linder demonstrated a remarkable ability to adjust quickly to difficult situations or sudden changes. Because of this, he was often able to snatch victory from the much clichéd jaws of defeat. One time , when the outlaw he had drawn sent him clear enough of the saddle for the judges to mark him down as eliminated — even the radio announcer shouted, "too bad, he's gone!" — Herman regained that old heaving deck and rode to the day's victory.

In Madison Square Garden in that banner year of 1933, a bucking horse named Old Mexico that had failed to buck all through the show and seemed about to hang up his hooves as a rodeo horse, suddenly exploded, almost catching Herman off guard. But not quite.

"Every time he was drawn, he just crow-hopped around the arena," Herman chuckled, "so I didn't expect a thing. Well, sir, all at once he turned in and really bucked. He did everything but shed his hide! I recovered and made day money on him. I don't think that old horse every bucked again after that!"

If a horse could buck, Herman generally managed to ride it. Most of his spills came on horses that refused to buck, as indicated by this excerpt from a Boston paper: "Herman Linder of Cardston, Alberta, champion cowboy of Canada and one of the high point winners in the bronc contest at the Boston Gardens rodeo, has been thrown only twice in 156 rides this year. And both times the horses refused to buck. Free arm waving high, spurs hard against the horse's shoulder, Linder flew out of the chutes on these two occasions, ready and balanced for a stiff, jarring rocking buck the instant the gates opened. Instead, the

horses stopped dead in their tracks and Linder went overboard."

When Herman's career really got underway, he was
making up to $5,000 a year, sometimes even more, which
was a lot better than he could do on the farm.

For several years after that Herman was probably one
of the highest money winners in the saddle and bareback
bronc riding. By the mid-thirties, he was regularly grossing
from $5,000 to $8,000 a year. It may not sound like much
money today, but in the middle of the Great Depression it
was a fortune.

Mrs. Linder was especially bothered by the long hours
of travelling by car over dusty roads. They would make
about one hundred miles every three hours, then take a
short stop to rest before continuing their journey. Crossing
half a continent that way was a time-consuming business.

"That's why I liked the big rodeos the best, like
Boston and New York," she said. "It meant you could
settle down in one place for a week or two and there was
always something to do.

"And the boys (the riders) had everything so well set
up for them. There was this Colonel Johnson who ran
those shows — he wasn't what you'd call a friend of the
cowboys as it turned out later — but he really knew how to
promote a show. He had real discipline in his rodeo. All
the cowboys had to be there for the big pre-show parade
and what was called the Grand Entry. If you weren't there,
you had to pay a fine of five dollars, which was a lot of
money to lose for no reason.

"And you didn't dare go in there with just your levis
on, no sir. If you had your levis on, you had to wear chaps
over them."

The parades went right down the main streets of the
city to the city hall, stopping traffic all along the way.
Then there would be smaller parades to the various
hospitals. And everybody had to have a horse with a
matching saddle and blanket. Colonel Johnson was a
showman and he knew how to build up the interest of the

public. Before that first day of parades was over, everybody knew the rodeo was in town and what they could expect to see.

But Mrs. Linder has fond memories of some of the small towns too. Here it was more a case of remembering people who helped them when they had to live under some pretty trying circumstances.

Two of the small towns that stand out in her memory are Sidney, Iowa, and Burwell, Nebraska. Most of the troubles involved finding a place to stay. There were no motels in those days, just the odd tourist cabin, roughly-made affairs, much like a farm granary, with the two-by-four studding bare on the insides. And there were always more customers than there were units to accommodate them.

"Where we stayed in Sidney was just a private home," said Mrs. Linder. "Once we arrived to find them busy canning fruit so they could only spare us a small corner of their kitchen to cook our meals. What I remember most about that time is the heat. It was hot weather anyway, and the stoves being on for the canning made it that much worse! But those people were mighty kind to let us stay. They didn't seem to mind the crowding one bit."

As there was only one hotel in Sidney and it was always full, a lot of the cowboys used to live in tents. But the Linders never did, although they did have a trailer for a while.

The biggest problem at Sidney was getting meals. Huge crowds used to come to this rodeo because the town was close to several larger centers. At mealtimes, the local restaurants were so crowded there were just no available seats.

"That didn't bother us too much," said Mrs. Linder, "because we didn't use restaurants. We cooked our own food because we were saving all the money we could to buy cattle for our ranch. In fact, most of our rodeo people stayed out of the restaurants. The tourist cabins or shacks they lived in had stoves and a stack of wood was supplied, so most did their own cooking. The boys who didn't have

Young Herman at his first Calgary Stampede in 1929
The Calgary Herald

Canada Kid riding a steer,
Calgary Stampede, 1923
Glenbow-Alberta Institute

Herman Linder on the *Mariposa* in
Sydney harbor, Australia
Russell Roberts Ltd.

Herman Linder on Payday, Colorado Springs Rodeo, Co.

Doubleday

Herman Linder bulldogging a steer in Sydney, Australia

Sun Feature Bureau, Sydney

Herman Linder on Steel Grey
E. W. Cadman

Herman Linder on Wing, Frontier Days, Cheyenne, Wy., 1938
Out-West Photo, Cheyenne

Herman Linder on Easy Money
E. W. Cadman

Herman Linder calf roping
E. W. Cadman

Herman Linder had this photograph of Rimrock taken as evidence for the trial at Vancouver. The dark patch where the neck joins the shoulder is the disputed injury. The blood stain would not have been noticed on a dark-colored horse.
Herman Linder

Warner Linder calf roping at the Cardston Stampede
Warner Linder

Herman Linder on Cigarette
E. W. Cadman

Herman Linder on Easy Money
E. W. Cadman

Herman Linder steer riding
E. W. Cadman

Herman Linder bull riding at Calgary, Alta.
E. W. Cadman

Herman Linder was made a member of the Blood Tribe at Cardston in 1942, then a blood brother, and finally an honorary chief in 1950. He was given the name *Oonestaseesoo-Kaus,* meaning "calf shirt." The Kainai Chieftainship is the official body of honorary chiefs of the Blood Tribe.

Herman Linder

At left: Prince Philip, Princess Elizabeth, Herman Linder, and Mayor Don Mackay of Calgary, Alta., 1951
E. W. Cadman

Herman and Agnes Linder,
July 11, 1956
The Calgary Herald

Herman and Agnes beside the original Linder log home
The Calgary Herald

The Linder Ranch today
The Calgary Herald

Joe Bews at the Edmonton Rodeo, 1974
Edmonton Exhibition Photo by Marcinkoski

Chuck wagon race, Calgary Stampede
Calgary Exhibition and Stampede Association

**Herman Linder with
John Pratt, head of Expo 67's
Entertainment Section, March 1966**
The Calgary Herald

"Barn Scene" left to right: Dick Cosgrave, Clem Gardner, Herman Linder and Pete Knight (kneeling).
Glenbow-Alberta Institute

Tom Bews at the Calgary Stampede, 1972
Edmonton Exhibition Photo by Dave Murphy

Jordie Thompson at Edmonton Rodeo, 1976
Edmonton Exhibition Photo by Marcinkoski

Herman Linder in his trophy room at his Cardston, Alta. ranch
The Calgary Herald

wives with them, or who weren't married, would eat with
the rest. I'd always have two or three boys in to dinner. We
were just one big family!"

Another problem on the road was keeping your clothes
clean. There were no laundromats, so every time they
stopped, the rodeo wives found themselves busy washing
out a pair of socks or a shirt. The cowboys never sent their
clothes to a laundry, and few of the small towns had a
laundry in any case.

"I did a lot of washing for the boys," Mrs. Linder
recalled. "I had to wash Herman's things anyway and one
or two extra didn't matter. The first thing you did when
you arrived in a new place was get your laundry done,
then you washed out the cupboards in your cabin and put
your food in. We always carried a grub box with us."

What were the hardest towns on the circuit for the
travelling rodeo riders? For the Linders they were
Cheyenne, Wyoming, and Pendleton, Oregon, said Mrs.
Linder.

"To us, our hardest times were spent in those two
towns," she said. "You had to compete against poor
contest judges. You were judged by who knew you. In fact,
when Pete Knight first went down there he rode for about
two years before anybody even saw him. Then after that,
you couldn't beat him. Pete never got any gifts from rodeo
— he had to really earn everything he got."

The Linders didn't have any children when Herman
was travelling the rodeo circuit. Although most of the
couples were childless because rodeo is a young man's
game, there were a few exceptions who did bring their
offspring along. Many wives stayed at home while their
husbands were on the road; others came for a short while ,
then went home.

"It was different with me," Mrs. Linder said. "The
rodeos were mostly down in the central or southern part of
the States and it was a long way from Cardston. When the
season was over, I was always glad to get back home.
Then, after I'd been home for a while I'd begin to miss the
travelling. You see, like Herman, my friends were on the

road too. I got to know those rodeo women really well and many of them are still close friends. Your ties are always strong with the friends you made when you were younger."

CHAPTER EIGHT

BUCK JUMPERS IN BRITAIN

Ever since Buffalo Bill's great Wild West Show had appeared in London years ago, the cowboy image had been strong in England. In 1934, The Tex Austin cowboy troupe was invited over there to put on a bronco busting show and Herman Linder and a few other Canadian riders were asked to go along.

The troupe was to travel on the liner *Aurania* and each member was supposed to pay his or her own way. Mrs. Linder didn't go with Herman on this trip because they were trying to save as much money as they could to build up their farm.

"Not many of our boys wanted to gamble the return fare on the chance of winning some money, so we were given a chance to go along with the rodeo stock," said Herman. "The rodeo promoters wanted to make sure they had at least some Canadian riders in their show."

Herman even worked his way to the embarkation point on the stock train. The pay of five dollars a day, plus meals was, in 1934, as good a deal as you'd find anywhere.

Because he was on the stock boat, Herman missed a little misadventure that befell the rest of the group. As the liner *Aurania* was proceeding down the St. Lawrence River from Montreal to Quebec City, she scraped her hull on some rocks as she was passing Cap du Sante. The impact caused slight leaks in tanks No. 2, 3, and 8, but the divers who inspected her hull said the damage was not serious and the ship was allowed to continue her journey to Plymouth, Havre, and London.

One thing they learned on arrival was that no Briton would ever think of using such a crude and inaccurate term as "bronco busting". Good heavens, one does not "bust" a horse. You don't even break it. If you did, the R.S.P.C.A. would get after you and that would jolly well be the end of it. In fact, it almost was. The correct term is of course "buck jumping" derived from the fact that a good horse will buck and jump about as you attempt to ride it.

"We took over some of the best rodeo stock there was," Herman said. "The horse contractors were McCartney and Elliott and their string included the world famous Midnight and Five Minutes to Midnight. The cowboys were all top men too. Pete Knight was one of them."

Arrival of the 100 cowboys and cowgirls, plus some of the best bucking horses in North America, should have been advertised for weeks before the event so people could plan to attend the rodeo. But it wasn't, because the R.S.P.C.A. put pressure on the authorities to forbid all advertising. The only publicity had to come from newspaper accounts and naturally these appeared only after the events happened. The result was that the giant White City Stadium, which could seat over 100,000 people for a soccer match, had only about 3,000 spectators for each performance. Financially the show was a flop.

"The only people who knew we were there were those who saw us walking around with our big hats and fancy boots," said Herman "There was a gentleman named Lord Lonsdale who was one of the great sportsmen in England. I'm sure he had put money in our show, but even he couldn't do anything about the situation. Somebody lost a lot of money, that's for sure!

"The R.S.P.C.A. was so strong over there they wouldn't even let us rope an animal properly," he continued. "All they'd let us use was a breakaway rope that let loose the minute you stopped your horse. If a steer ever fell over accidentally, you were liable to find yourself in jail. For steer wrestling, they just put a band around the critter's belly with a ribbon on it, and you had to ride by and take it off. But they paid the money out on that basis and the money was good. In fact, right up to the time I turned my ankle, I had won almost $1,000."

The newspapers did what they could to help make the show a success by writing colorful and often humorous accounts of the various happenings. In a story entitled "Rodeo is Great Fun," writer Viscount Castlerosse even ridiculed the official attitude when he wrote: "Old women of both sexes shivered at the thought of the terrible things that could go on. They need not have done so. The rodeo is not cruel. Nothing like so cruel to the spectators as the test match, or to the horses as the ordinary ride in Rotten Row.

"As to the cowboys themselves, if you get a man as hard as nails, as brave as a lion and as active as a cat, as lithe as a serpent, then you have a cowboy. It is unnecessary to worry about the fate of cowboys, because something tells me that they would not enjoy a life which would involve being tucked up into bed with a glass of hot milk by their side. . . .

"The first cowboy I spoke to was Dogtown Slim," Viscount Castlerosse continued. "He comes from seventy miles off the Mexican border. He said to me, 'I've got a bad horse.' He was right. The contest consisted in riding buck jumpers bareback with no bridle. The rider had to keep one hand in the air and move his feet forward and back until the sound of the whistle. Mr. Slim's horse did everything except turn himself inside out and they parted company. I came to the conclusion that Mr. Slim could not be accused of exaggeration.

"Pete Knight of Calgary, winner of the Prince of Wales Trophy two years running, and I had a conversation. I said to him: 'In these contests it must make a difference if you get a good horse or a bad horse.' Mr. Knight nodded, and then as an afterthought he added: 'Of course, you've got to be able to ride your horse.' Shortly afterwards, I saw Mr.

Slim remain unmoved while a bronco alternatively stood
on its head and its tail. Apparently the announcer, after
one particularly savage buck jumper had unseated its
rider, remarked feelingly: 'I wish my mother-in-law was
riding that horse.' . . .

"As for the cowboys themselves, they are very much
the type that every reader of good literature expects. A
jollier little crew you never saw. Tex Austin is the type that
any woman novelist would make her hero, if she were
writing a cowboy story. . . .

"Rodeo is all right. That is, if you like to see men from
the wild and wooly West do things you wouldn't dare do
yourself. Halfway through the program, they played 'The
Last Roundup'. The cowboys took it nobly without
flinching."

In a story dated May 28th, 1934, a South Wales paper,
the *Echo and Express* ran a story about the landing of the
rodeo stock at the Cardiff docks. "Take it from me," says
the writer, "there are other and better ways of earning a
living than being nurse and valet to 250 half-wild horses.
Not counting 150 singularly vicious steers. Still, twenty-
one real he-man cowboys did it at Cardiff Docks, Sunday
evening when the steamship *Nortonian* got in with the
advance guard of a rodeo which is to be staged in London
next month. What was more, they seemed to like doing
it.

"Small boys climbed the fences around the cattle lairs
to catch a glimpse of these heroes. They shouted with
delight: 'Ride 'em cowboy!'

"Young cowboys they were, all gleaming teeth, silk
shirts, high-heeled boots and jeans. You know, Tom Mix,
or William Farnum, the sort who used to fire twenty shots
from a Colt without reloading and rescue the heroine from
a fate worse than death, whatever that may be.

"But they made a good job of the unloading. Steers
with horns as long as mother-in-laws weekend stay shot up
from the hold and down a gangway to the quayside. The
boys just encouraged them in their usual way when things
looked a little nastier than usual. Then they brought up the

horses. I don't like the beasts myself, never have, never shall. But there was beauty in these, though. Sleek, their coats were like silk. They sniffed the air as they came on deck, some were frightened and shied, but the boys gentled them.

" 'Say Bo,' said a cowboy, 'they won't bite.' "

The writer of the news report apparently didn't believe the cowboy, for his story continues:

"Wouldn't they? Wouldn't they! One cayuse — there, I knew that Western thriller would come in use one day — took a dislike to its mate. It planted two heavy hooves into its side and snickered. A gray came up too qickly. Horseplay! The cowboy who had told me they wouldn't bite moved out of the way quickly enough. . . .

"Yet strangely enough the unloading was quiet. There was no shouting or excitement, such as one anticipated. 'What's the point of it?' remarked Clark Lund, champion cowboy out of somewhere in the West, 'They'd only get excited too and an excited horse can sure be tough'."

The writer ended his account here, but it's plain to see the arrival of Herman Linder and his fellow cowhands on the ship that carried the rodeo stock was quite an event in Cardiff.

Herman was doing very well right up until he had the bad luck to turn his ankle. Like a lot of his accidents, it didn't come while he was riding a bucking bronc.

"This horse didn't even buck a jump," he recalled. "It just kind of ran out there and turned around a bit. When the pick-up men went to take me off, the horse would spin around this way and that way. So I just stepped off him and that's when I turned my foot. I must have really twisted my ankle because in an hour or so my foot was swollen right up to my knee.

"Well, I didn't feel like quitting right off because I had one more good bareback drawn for the next round, which would be that evening. But I decided one more ride was all I'd make. I felt that if I kept on competing right to the end I would just make it worse, so I went down that afternoon and booked passage back home on the *Empress of Britain*.

Pat Burton decided he wasn't doing any good over their either, so he booked passage with me.

"That night at the rodeo, I got a boot from somebody — a shoe boot. You know, the kind that lace up — it was about two sizes bigger than I usually wear. Then I had a shot of cocaine, or something, put into the foot to kill the pain. I laced that boot on and put a spur on it and won the day money. You feel better if you can end with a win."

Next morning, Herman and fellow rider, Pat Burton, left aboard the big C.P.R. liner for Canada. When he reached home, Herman had only two weeks to get ready for the Calgary Stampede, injured foot or not. That was the year he won just about everything in sight at the famous show!

"As far as I know, that was it for rodeo in England," said Herman. "They've never had a rodeo since. But I enjoyed my trip over, in spite of the bad luck with my foot. There were some Campbells who rodeod here in Canada. They wrote to their relatives there to say we were coming over. One of their uncles picked me up, along with some of the other Canadian riders, and took us all over the place.

"Of course, we were down to Buckingham Palace to see the Changing of the Guard. We also saw the Epsom Downs Derby race. They took several busloads of cowboys out to this Derby. What a sight that was! I think that was the biggest mass of people I ever saw in my life. It's too bad we couldn't have had a crowd like that at our rodeo.

"We had beautiful space right in front of the grandstand, almost at the finish line. You could see the glassed-in place where the King and Queen were and see them moving around. That Derby is something I will never forget!"

Herman's outstanding memory of the London rodeo was the attendance of hundreds of school children who had been brought in from all over England especially to see it. This was surprising when so many adults in Great

Britain seemed to believe rodeo was an inhumane spectacle.

Later, the children were asked by their teachers to write a composition on what they had witnessed. If the teachers expected them to condemn rodeo, they were sadly disillusioned, for without exception their charges wrote that they were disappointed none of the cowboys carried a gun, and that there were no Indians. These kids had been brought up on a diet of Western movies and penny-dreadful thrillers.

"At that time, many people in the Old Land still thought of North America as over-run with Indians and cowboys popping away with six guns at every opportunity," Herman laughed. "I never carried a gun in my life. For one thing, it's against the law. And it would sure be dangerous, because all the other cowboys would die laughing if they saw you walking around toting one!"

CHAPTER NINE

IT ONLY HURTS WHEN YOU LAUGH

Smashed ribs go hand in hand with bronco busting, but it only hurts when you laugh, as some wag once said. Getting Herman to admit he was ever hurt while riding is like trying to put socks on an octopus — no matter how hard you press you get nowhere. He is inclined to make light of the whole business, which leaves you with the impression he'd only admit to a serious injury if he were hung up in the reins, drawn by a slipped bareback rigging, and quartered by the bronc's flailing hooves.

In fact, he was pretty badly hurt several times: once in Boston and once at the Calgary Stampede. But his most serious injury of all came after he had stopped competing as a rider. Another time he was almost put out of action by a circular saw while cutting wood on the farm. And once he saw a rider killed at a rodeo, but he won't talk about that either.

Mrs. Linder recalls the Boston accident as a very anxious time because they were a long way from home and she didn't know how they'd be able to get their car back if they had to go by train.

"It happened in his second last performance," she said. "I was at the hotel packing, because after the evening performance we would be through and we wanted to be ready to start out the next morning early. There was a sudden knock on the door and I opened it to find one of

the boys standing there with a worried look on his face.
Then he blurted out that Herman was badly hurt and I
had better get over to the hospital as quickly as I could.
From then on until we got to Herman's bedside I hardly
knew what I was doing, I was so worried.

"They said he had two or three ribs just clipped right
off his backbone, but the way it turned out it wasn't as
serious as we had thought. It did delay us for quite a while,
but one of the Alberta boys named Jackie Cooper, stayed
right there with us and then helped us drive back home.
Rodeo people are like that — ready to pitch in and give
you a hand when you're in trouble."

At the time of his accident, Herman Linder was a big
star in Boston and the newspaper reporters made much of
his accident, writing in the colorful prose of that day.

Said one headline on November 13th, 1935: "Herman
Linder, The Alberta Horse Tamer Slept Well Last Night."
Then the story went on to say: "Linder, star member of a
rodeo performance here, suffered a couple of broken ribs
Monday night when tossed from the back of Big Boy. . . .
Hospital attaché at first feared that his chest was crushed
last night when a notoriously bad acting bay, Big Boy,
tossed him heavily to the tanbark. Linder had been a top
performer for years all over North America."

Another paper headed its story "Little Busted Buster,"
and played up the role of Mrs. Linder in her husband's
recovery. The story read: "Mrs. Linder has a big job here.
She's got to get her husband well. Of course, doctors and
nurses will help, but a big factor on the road to recovery
for Herman Linder, bronco rider, who was flung from his
steed Monday night at Boston Gardens, will be the loving
care of his wife."

And today Herman is quick to agree with that version
of it. Through all his years on the road he was thankful to
have his wife with him to share the good times and the
bad.

Writer Dorothy G. Weyman has described the accident
and the courage of those involved: "The cowboys tried to
help every way they could. They stood around Herman's

unconscious body in the arena blocking off the wild attack
of the vicious bronco. Fanning Herman ineffectively with
their ten gallon sombreros — it was all they could think of
to do and they had to do something. There was big Dick
Shelton and John Bowman, the pickup men who would
have given an arm if they could have reached Herman in
time to snatch him from those stamping hooves.

"There was Jimmy Nesbitt and Jaspo Fulkerson the
clowns, smearing the paint on their faces with fingers that
brushed something from smarting eyes. Shorty Hill picked
up Herman's chaps and sombrero when they lifted him on
the stretcher for the ambulance ride. John Jordan, the
good-looking announcer had a frog in his throat when he
tried to go on with the show."

Mrs. Linder was not in the arena at the time. She was
soon to go into hospital for an operation, and Herman was
riding in the rodeo to win the prize money for her hospital
bills. Miss Weyman describes the concern for Mrs. Linder:
"First thing the other cowboys thought of even when they
were lifting Herman's unconscious broken body from the
tanbark and carrying it off in the stretcher, was his wife.
Big and brawny and tough as steel these bronc-busting
men, but they're shy when women come in. Owen Wister
knew them so well in his book *The Virginian.* One of the
cowboys came running in to ask me if I would stand by
Herman's wife, so I rode in the ambulance and waited at
the hospital with her, and I saw two people with
magnificent courage and affection for each other. She
(Mrs. Linder) was white as skim-milk and shaking like a
leaf, but she held her chin up and kept back her tears and
said, 'I've got to smile for Herman, or he'll think he's hurt
real bad'.

"There was Agnes and I sitting in the waiting room
while upstairs doctors and nurses did things for Herman.
Then the nurse came to say Agnes could go upstairs. They
took one look at the girl's drawn white face and said to me,
'You'd better go with her in case she keels over'. But she
didn't keel over. She went in with a smile like it was
Christmas day and she leaned over and kissed him saying,

'You'll feel better in the morning. I'll be back in the morning after you have a good sleep.' "

Then as Herman began to mend, there were more Boston headlines such as: "Herman Linder Leaves Hospital." Although this was only the third year the rough riding cowboys had appeared at Boston, the city had now taken rodeo to its heart and a great deal of that affection and esteem centered on Herman Linder. The fans had marked him out for special attention since that first show in 1933 when the city elite had come down for a Western meal with the riders.

Later, Herman broke a wrist while riding in New York, but he doesn't even count that as an accident. Even the big city's newspapers made light of his injury as witness the account of one evening paper: "If Herman Linder wasn't crippled with a fractured wrist, he probably would ride comets and shooting stars for amusement. However, the gangling cowboy from Cardston, Alberta, has only the one good hand at the moment and has to curtail his activities to keep him in the world champion rodeo holding forth in Madison Square Garden. The wrist he cracked up in a spill at an early edition of the show in no way cramped his style last night when he took first money in the bareback riding contest. He really bent a pesky bucker called Mill Iron to his will and remained aboard eight seconds, a better showing than any one of the ten other competitors were able to turn in, and with his left wrist broken."

"It was always a relief, though, when the riding was over and you saw that everyone was safe," Mrs. Linder said. "I guess in your mind you were expecting something bad to happen."

Once at the Calgary Stampede, Herman got a kick in the face which could have killed him. Mrs. Linder remembers that accident as another anxious moment that had her wondering if Herman would ever make it into retirement.

"Herman was riding bareback," she said, "and the picket man jumped in front of his horse. The horse dodged and the unexpected movement threw Herman so he landed half under the big, rough planks of the corral fence. Luckily there wasn't a plank at that particular place and I think it was the only thing that saved him. The horse kicked Herman right in the jaw and he rode eight rerides after that, one after the other, and couldn't remember riding one of them."

Commenting on this mishap, a write-up in the *Calgary Herald* said: "For a short time in the early part of the final contest Saturday afternoon it looked as though Herman Linder would not be able to finish out the Stampede in which he held a lead in several events. The Cardston cowboy, jumping from the horse at the end of his original ride in the Canadian Bronc Riding, got a kick in the face which knocked him unconscious and cut open his chin. He received medical aid on the grounds and, though groggy for some time, was eventually able to complete all of his scheduled rides. He was forced to pass up his final calf in the Calf Roping event, however."

The Calf Roping title went to another member of the Linder family, who was also badly injured. With a broken collar bone and ligaments torn from his back, brother Warner Linder tied a calf in fast time that day to capture the Canadian Championship. And Warner didn't leave it at that. In spite of the fact that he was all bound up in a T-splint, he performed the most spectacular feat of that year's show by making a flying tackle at a steer to set a world's record for consecutive wins in Wild Steer Decorating.

Bronco busters and steer wrestlers have a hard time getting any insurance. When asked about this during his riding career, Herman admitted that for some strange reason, life insurance salesmen never seem to pester him. Not a cent of insurance had he been able to get since he was a boy of sixteen but he intended to change all that when he retired.

At one time, newspapers were speculating that he might have to retire early because of an accident on the farm: "Herman Linder may never ride broncos again," said one write-up. "He is lying in the Cardston Hospital suffering with a finger cut badly with a circular saw. The accident occurred at the Herman Linder farm when sawing wood for the farm house. His finger was cut just at the knuckle joint. Determined to save it if he could, Herman had the doctor sew it on again and it is yet doubtful if he can save the finger."

But the Boston mishap was the most serious injury of Herman's riding career and there was an interesting sequel to it. When he returned to Bean City the following year, Herman learned that the management of Boston Gardens had given the rodeo producer Colonel Johnson $100 to give to Herman to help with his hospital expenses. "I never did collect that money," Herman laughed.

The year of the accident, Herman parted company with his bucking horse, old Pardner, and the new owner was that same Colonel Johnson. The Colonel owned some of the toughest bucking horses in the business and he claimed they were the best in the country. Herman told him he had a real bucking horse which he could have for $250. What's more, he was guaranteed to buck, and if he didn't prove to be one of the top horses in Johnson's string he wouldn't have to pay Herman anything.

Naturally Johnson took him up on it and Pardner started out on a journey that was to take in the top shows of the Continent. At this time, the gelding was fifteen years old and as gentle as the mist that falls on the high grass range — until you put him in a chute, that is.

The first stop was at Indianapolis for a two-week show, then on to New York and Madison Square Garden. After that, came Boston for another two-week show. In that time, Pardner was successfully ridden only three times, dumping some of the best riders in the world. But Herman never did collect all of that $250 from the wiley promoter either.

Two years later, Pardner's picture appeared on a rodeo program and he was listed in the top ten horses of the string. They had now changed his name to Schoolboy Rowe.

"If he'd gotten into rodeo right away and into a string of bucking horses like Midnight did in 1925, he'd have gone down in history as one of the greatest bucking horses," Herman said. "I figure I've had a lot of experience riding tough horses, but I was never on a tougher horse than Pardner!"

CHAPTER TEN

THE JACKAROO TRAIL

The year 1936 was a memorable one for Herman Linder. In January, he crossed the Pacific to compete in a big rodeo held in Sydney, Australia where they call a cowboy a "Jackaroo".

If only Herman had been born in Michigan instead of a few miles away in Wisconsin, he might have been able to bill himself as the "Jackaroo from Kalamazoo". As it was, he had to be content to put himself down as just Herman Linder from Cardston, Alberta. But this must have been quite satisfactory to the Australians for they lost no time in inviting him to come back in 1938 for another round of buck jumping.

Like their British forebears, Australians prefer "buck jumping" to "bronco busting". In North America, we obtained a lot of our cowboy terms from the Spanish. The sport itself, "rodeo" stands for a roundabout course, or a roundup, and comes from the Spanish verb *rodear,* which means to "go around". The word "bronco" means "rough" or "wild" in Spanish, and, of course, "ranch" is derived from *rancho.*

The Australians had to make up most of their own names. For instance, instead of someone going to a rodeo to watch cowboys ride broncos, Australians go to a "Bushman's Carnival" to watch "jackaroos buck jumping". And you don't visit a cattle ranch down there — you go to a "cattle station". But their contests are just as exciting for the spectators and just as hard on the tailbone if you happen to be one of the riders.

For the Linders, getting to Australia was half the fun because they set out from San Francisco that first January on an old packet of the Union Royal Mail Line named the *Makura*. She was a small ship of only 8,075 tons and this was to be her last trip as a passenger vessel on that route. She was twenty-eight years old and held the world mileage record of three million miles. Later that year, she was sold as scrap metal to Japan.

The Linders and the rest of the cowboy troupe booked on her because regular passenger ships didn't stop at all the South Sea Island ports that the *Makura* visited and the cowboys wanted to see all they could. It wasn't a case of having to keep down expenses this time because their Australian sponsors had footed the bill for their passage. All living expenses were provided as well as $400 in cash for each competitor.

On the first trip over, Warner Linder accompanied Herman and competed in some of the events. There were nine performers in the party all told: eight cowboys and a clown. Four of the riders were Canadian, and the rest were American. In addition, there were two women — Mrs. Linder and the wife of one of the American boys. On the second trip in 1938, Mrs. Linder was the only woman along.

"In those days, Tahiti was in its natural state," said Herman, "a really beautiful place. And from there we went over to Rarotonga. We had to anchor off shore there and go in on boats. It was quite a thing to see! They loaded many many cases of bananas and those natives worked like mad to get the loading done on time. We just had twelve hours in each place."

The journey from San Francisco until the *Makura* docked in Sydney, Australia, took twenty-four days. On the first leg out across the Pacific to the Islands the passengers didn't sight land for nineteen days.

Although she had never been on a ship before, Mrs. Linder didn't find the trip monotonous and she didn't get seasick. Maybe one of the main reasons was that she managed to keep busy most of the way.

"Oh, I'll admit I felt a bit woozy a couple of times," she laughed, "but I was never down with it. They had a third class on that ship, but we weren't in it. If we had been, maybe we'd all have gotten sick. There were some young auto-racers travelling at the same time and they were in third class. I sure felt sorry for those kids because they had a pretty rough time of it stuck away down in the bottom of the ship.

"I did the washing for the whole rodeo bunch," she continued. "Every one of the boys had twelve white shirts so I had to clean them every day."

But the trip was never tedious because they had games of all sorts. You didn't have time to get lonesome or homesick. They had some competitions and costume parties and the night before they landed anywhere there would be a big party.

"You know, I'm glad I saw the South Seas before it became commercialized. I always said if God ever made a paradise on this earth, it was Rarotonga."

Like the "Ruler of the Queen's Navy" of H.M.S. *Pinafore,* Herman was never sick at sea either. Well, hardly ever. There was one time just after the old packet steamed away from New Zealand when he and his dinner abruptly parted company. And even then he escaped blame.

"We had come all the way to New Zealand with only twenty-four passengers," said Herman, "but there we took on about 300. Soon after we left Auckland, the weather started to blow up, and boy, were those new passengers sick! Members of our group were the only ones who came down to dinner.

"But after dinner, I began to feel a bit woozy in my stomach too, so I headed for our stateroom. Just as I turned to go into the passage between the staterooms, I suddenly lost all my meal. After that I felt fine, so I rushed into my stateroom and washed my face off. I had just opened the door to go out again when around the corner came one of the stewards. He looked down at the mess on the deck and shook his head.

"Somebody sure must have been awful sick!" I said.

"It's those people in the next cabin," the steward nodded, "they've been sick ever since we left harbor."

"Guess they haven't got their sea legs yet," said Herman, as one old sea dog to another, and went away chuckling to himself. The steward never did find out who the real culprit was.

In Australia, the rodeo troupe was met by officials of the Royal Agricultural Society, sponsors of an annual fair at Sydney that is one of the largest fairs in the world. As entertainers in the big show, the North Americans were treated royally. Riding horses and rodeo stock were provided for them and they were given six weeks out on one of the cattle stations, about 250 miles from Sydney, to train the animals for the event.

On the trip to cattle country, the North Americans found themselves the center of attention once more. Drinks were passed freely around the train. By the time the cowboys had transferred to the branch line that would take them on their final leg, nobody was feeling any pain — least of all Oral Zumalt, one of the U.S. riders.

Zumalt climbed into the cab with the engineer, who soon warmed to the occasion enough to let the cowboy take over the controls. Oral turned up the speed and they found themselves zooming wildly around tight curves with the whistle blowing madly.

Herman leaned out a window to see what was happening and away went his prized sombrero in a gust of wind, tumbling across the bare, dry countryside like a thing alive until it finally disappeared from sight. When they reached their destination, Herman asked the train crew if they would keep an eye out for his hat on their way back, which they promised to do.

"In this country, the wind blows back and forth across the track," the conductor assured him. "We'll probably see it again."

By the time the group was ready to return to Sydney some six weeks later, the hat still hadn't been recovered.

"But I didn't give up on it," said Herman. "When we reached the spot where I lost it I had everybody keep their eyes open and, sure enough, there it came blowing across the tracks like a tumbleweed. The engineer obligingly stopped the train and I jumped out and got it."

During their stay at the cattle station, the cowboys were sent some beautiful horses to work with. "They sent a whole carload of them," Herman recalled. "We were told to pick one horse apiece out of the whole bunch. Of course, these horses had never been roped off of, or even jumped from for steer wrestling. They had just been ridden with the flat saddle. And Australians ride their horses with the rein in each hand — drive them, that is — so the horses needed to be trained for rodeo work."

The rodeo group was quartered at one of the small stations, but did the horse training at a larger one. There they were given a paddock to practise in and a bunch of steers, or bullocks as Australians call them, to work with. Herman and his cohorts played around there for over a month just doing the things they liked best, which was roping and riding.

While the boys were busy training their horses, the women had plenty of time to look about and see what it was like to live on a cattle station. "The country didn't seem a bit strange," said Mrs. Linder. "It was dry and reminded me a lot of California. We found there were only two classes of people out there at that time, the rich and the poor. The place we stayed at was one of the poorer ones, but the people were just marvelous to us. They didn't have such things as screens on doors and windows and there were flies all over the place. But the people themselves were very clean and careful. The minute a dish of food was set down before you it was covered with a net — nothing was left uncovered.

"But on the big wealthy estates, like the one where the boys did their training, it was another story. They had big screened-in areas. Because we were from North America, we were invited by the lords and ladies who owned these places to attend social events there. One of them, the estate of Lord and Lady McMaster, was just gorgeous! I was told they had all the films shown at their place before the rest of Australia ever got to see them. For that purpose they had a well-equipped theater right in their home."

The Australians have regular strings of bucking horses to use in their buck jumping contests. And they are certainly tough to ride, as Herman found the first time he mounted one. They were small, but tricky.

"Their horses may have been small compared to ours," he said, "but they sure bucked, mind you! They really had a lot of action and were very catty. They would swap ends quick as you please, but they didn't have the power our big horses have. I don't think any of them weighed over 800 to 900 pounds."

When they went to Sydney for the big show, Mrs. Linder prepared the food for the Canadian cowboys. In the huge arena provided for them, the riders found one hazard they hadn't counted on: the water jumps and broad jump barriers for the horse shows were permanent fixtures. But it was really only a mental hazard for the arena was so big there was no serious problem.

"One thing that took a bit of getting used to was the flat English riding saddles we had to use," said Herman, "and there was a little roll, maybe an inch and a half high, that your leg was up against all the time.

"But the bucking strap, or flank strap as we call it, used over there was made of leather and had a sheepskin cover. The way it's put together, you put it on real loose and when the horse leaves the chute you just hang on. It pulls itself up tight and sort of locks. Does that sound familiar? Of course it does, because we brought it back from Australia in 1936 and it's used 100 percent in all the rodeos in the United States and Canada now!

"I don't know who developed it over there. It's a very simple thing when you come to think of it, but I'll bet you there isn't a cowboy today who knows where that strap came from. Better still, I'll bet you there isn't even one rodeo producer today with a string of bucking horses who knows where that strap came from!"

When the show was over, the bronco busters left Australia on the 22.5-knot, 19,000-ton Matson liner *Mariposa* for San Francisco. Being bigger and faster than the ship they had come over on — and making fewer stops — the *Mariposa* made the return trip in nineteen days.

For the second trip over in 1938, the Linders sailed out of Vancouver, B.C. on the M.V. *Aorangi,* at that time, the world's largest motor ship — a forerunner of the big diesel and diesel electric ships. This trip was made via Hawaii and also took just nineteen days, because, like the *Mariposa*, the big, green-hulled vessel was fast.

"We went to the same small cattle station as before," said Mrs. Linder. "It was really nice to see our friends again, but the country was in a bad drought that year. It was dusty and hot and we scarcely had enough drinking water."

At the rodeo show that year four New Zealand cowboys were entered in the contests. "Those boys had a rough time of it," Herman smiled. "They got bucked off every day they rode. I don't think any of them ever rode a horse to the finish. Like I said, those Australian horses can be tough."

They again made the return trip on the liner *Mariposa,* sailing by way of New Zealand, Fiji, Samoa, and the Hawaiian Islands. After they landed at San Francisco, Herman started riding in a few rodeos in California. The Linders would have liked to have stayed for a while, but Herman got a call from Cardston saying the town was putting on its Golden Jubilee show, for which they wanted their big star back home.

The Linders have many happy memories of their two visits Down Under, plus a couple of cups awarded for Herman's prowess in the "International Buck Jumping Contest". Canadian and United States rodeos also have a bucking strap that has won wide acceptance everywhere — well, almost everywhere. At one point in Herman's unfolding career that bucking strap was destined to figure in a case that saw Herman hauled all the way to the Supreme Court.

CHAPTER ELEVEN

THE COWBOY TURTLES

The year of the first Australian trip saw the birth of the Cowboy Turtles. The cowboys called their first organization the Cowboy Turtle Association, not because the cowboy himself is slow of body and mind — he couldn't be or he wouldn't survive — but because he is an independent soul who is slow to take group action. He prefers to act alone.

But there comes a time when group action is the only answer. For the cowboys, that time came on November 3, 1936, in the Boston Gardens when they went on strike for better working conditions. As one of the leading performers, Herman Linder was naturally in the forefront of the action.

"This trouble had been building up for many years," Linder explained. "The only rodeo organization at that time was the Rodeo Association of America, which was set up at Salinas, California in 1929. But this outfit spoke mostly for the rodeo managers. The cowboy was just considered incidental to the show. He had to travel great distances at his own expense in the hope of winning some prize money and he had to put up an entry fee just to get into the contest. At some shows, the prize money being offered wasn't much more than the combined entry fees. In other words, the cowboys were risking their necks to win back their own money. You can get better odds than that in any poker game.

"Take Hugh Bennett, for instance," Herman continued. "He was one of the top money winners in the States. He travelled all the way from his ranch in Arizona to attend the Boston show, won two championship events, yet he cleared only $350."

The big issue at the Boston strike was the smallness of the prize money offered. The cowboys wanted their entry fees added to the purse and they also wanted the prize money to be increased by $4,000. The show was attracting huge crowds and they figured the performers that the crowds came to see should have a bigger share of the profits.

The show's promoter, the inevitable Colonel W. T. Johnson, thought differently and reacted in typical fashion. He decided he would just ignore the loss of sixty-one top performers and put on the show with those he had on contract and a varied assortment of grooms and pick-up men.

"We are going to put on a first class show," he announced to the press. "Yes sir, just as good a show as has ever been staged in Boston! We have plenty of riders en route from Chicago where they have just finished up a rodeo."

But the strikers had received assurances in writing from the 130 to 135 contestants in the Chicago show that they had no intention of coming to Boston as strike-breaking cowboys. The riders could see there was a big issue at stake and they decided to let the drama unfold, as indeed it did.

The strikers were very skeptical of Johnson's claims he could put on a top show without them and they decided they'd pay their way into the evening performance and see what happened.

"Johnson still has a few good riders," Hugh Bennett admitted to the press, "but not very many. The girls in the show are not on strike because they're all on contract. Some of the fellas who are on contract will have to ride too because they have an obligation to Johnson. But if any others try it, we'll see they don't ride in many other rodeos!" he added grimly.

Another point of contention was that earlier in the day Colonel Johnson had fired one of the contest judges, Bob Crosby. Good, experienced cowboy judges were few and far between and the strikers said they wouldn't return unless Crosby was reinstated. Crosby, who was holder of the Theodore Roosevelt Trophy, emblematic of the All-Around Cowboy Championship at the Pendleton, Oregon, and Cheyenne, Wyoming rodeos for three years running, had defied the blustering Colonel by insisting on riding in the Grand Entry parade after he had been discharged. Crosby said he had a contract with the rodeo and he was going to honor it, no matter what Johnson did. The Colonel had also fired two of his pick-up men who expressed sympathy for the strikers.

Among the strikers were many of the top names in rodeo of the day. In addition to Herman Linder, they included: Pete Knight, many times World Champion Bronc Rider; Everett Shaw, winner of the Calf Roping in New York two weeks previously; Everett Bowman, R.A.A. Champion All-Around Cowboy for 1935; John Bowman, points leader for that trophy that year; Herbert Meyers, many times Champion Calf Roper; Eddie Curtis, winner of the Denver Bronc Riding contest the year before; Hub Whiteman, famed bronc fighter, and our own Canada Kid.

Before the evening's performance, the strikers had one of their number dressed up in ordinary city duds go to the box office and pick up a bunch of ringside tickets. It was the first time these champions had ever watched a rodeo event from the public stands. In silence they waited for the final announcement which signalled the start of the Grand Entry. This was a flowery introduction of their opponent, Colonel Johnson.

As Johnson came riding forward to the center of the arena, the sixty-one waiting cowboys let out such an outcry of shouting and booing the announcer's voice was

drowned in the din. The band suddenly launched into
"The Star-Spangled Banner", which brought the cowboys
to their feet out of respect for the anthem and delayed the
demonstration for a few minutes. But the Band couldn't go
on saluting Old Glory forever. Then, under the strain, the
band leader must have temporarily lost his sanity or
control for he led his crew into a brilliant rendition of
"Empty Saddles in the Old Corral."

This was too much for the cowboys who immediately
joined in, bellowing the words lustily. Amid great laugh-
ter, the delighted crowd accompanied them, filling the
cavernous arena with a swelling bedlam of sound. Now in
utter confusion, the band hastily switched to a less
appropriate tune, but the damage was done. Arena
officials could see they were in for a noisy evening. Led by
Sergeant Michael Carr, a strong detachment of Boston's
finest was summoned to keep order to prevent those
bronco busting spalpeens from wrecking the show.

For a moment an uneasy quiet reigned, then the
announcer, John Jordan, called the Bronc Riding events
and the strikers started booing again. Their hoots, howls,
and catcalls continued for a solid hour until Sergeant Carr
warned that he'd eject every living man of them if they
didn't pipe down and behave themselves.

"I appreciate the point you boys are trying to make,"
he told Herman, "but I can't go on ignoring such a wild
disturbance forever, you understand."

Herman understood enough to know they wouldn't do
their cause much good by spending the night in jail, so he
and some of the other strike leaders finally prevailed on
their cohorts to tone down their demonstration.

Except for an occasional shout of "Bring on the
cowboys!" and "When are you going to show us some
riders", the strikers watched in grim amusement while
grooms from the stables, chute men and roustabouts, who
had never seriously competed for prize money, came
thundering into the arena uneasily perched on heaving
broncs. For good measure, Colonel Johnson threw in Wild
West actors and pick-up men. Rider after rider was

promptly bucked off, or failed to make a qualified ride. The 3,000-odd spectators grew disgusted.

Finally, the crowd took a hand and began to chant, "Show us some riders, show us some riders!" and Colonel Johnson knew he was beaten. He called striker spokesman Everett Bowman over to him and agreed to meet all their demands.

"How about giving us that in writing," one of the leaders said, and again the Colonel agreed.

While the strike was on, Boston Gardens manager, George B. Brown, had thrown open the books to the strikers to show that the Garden didn't make a big killing on rodeos.

Examining last year's figures, Herman came across an item that read: "Herman Linder, $100." Brown explained that he gave the money to Johnson to help with Herman's hospital expenses when he was hurt the previous year.

When Herman tackled the Colonel about it, the latter claimed he gave Herman $100.

"That $100 was a downpayment on old Pardner," Herman pointed out, but the Colonel said $100 was $100. Between the gift from the Gardens and the sale of Pardner, Herman ended up $250 short.

At the suggestion of George Brown, Johnson did agree that all cowboys who paid money to watch the events should be given $20 apiece on turning in their ticket stubs to him. The whole group retired to a small office overlooking the arena to settle the details of their new demands.

The cowboy demands were presented by a committee representing various events. Steer wrestlers had Hub Whiteman for their spokesman and the calf ropers had Bob Crosby. Acting for the saddle bronc riders was Eddie Curtis, for the bareback riders, Dick Griffith, and the bull rider spokesman was Paul Carney.

The strikers wanted total prize money of $15,200 for the week's competition, but Johnson wasn't prepared to go so far. After lengthy negotiations, he agreed to add $4,000 to the existing $7,000 purse and to give back $1,500 in

entry fees. Garden manager Brown added another $1,250.
The Colonel also agreed to reinstate Bob Crosby and the
two pick-up men he had fired.

Just as the crusty old rodeo promoter was about to sign
the new agreement, a new spate of booing broke from the
stands where the rest of the strikers were sitting. The
Colonel looked out to find that somebody was booing his
beloved white pony, Old Buck. Enraged, the Colonel flung
down his pen. "Everything is off!" he shouted angrily and
marched out of the office.

This delay was too much for the cowboys. They ran
after him and told him if he didn't sign now they would all
leave town in the morning because there really wasn't
enough prize money in the show to make it worthwhile.

Finally, the Colonel relented and signed the fateful
paper which, with the return of the fees and the bonus
from the Garden management, would almost double the
original prize money.

Now peace was finally restored. To show their good
faith, the cowboys marched out into the arena with the
Colonel and announced to the audience they would be
back in the saddle for the next show. Then everybody had
a crack at speech making just to prove there were no hard
feelings and that the first cowboy strike wouldn't leave any
scars.

Said George Brown for the Gardens: "I am extremely
pleased at the outcome of the strike, for it means Boston
will be able to see the best cowboys in the world competing
in real contests." In that one evening, manager Brown had
apparently seen enough unreal contests to last him a lifetime.

Even Colonel Johnson was moved to eloquence by the
occasion. "The show will go on!" he told everybody. "We
will continue to put on the best rodeo in the country with
the best cowboys that ever rode for prize money." Then to
show he was a good sport, he continued, "I don't hold any
hard feelings against the men. The only way they have to
earn their living is by winning prize money. But," he
added, just to show that a rodeo manager's life wasn't any

bed of roses either, "sometimes they don't appreciate the difficulties of putting on a rodeo."

For the cowboys, Herman Linder said: "All we want is a fair share of the prize money. Now that is all settled, we'll be out here doing our best to win as every good rodeo contestant always does."

Newspapers all over the Continent had comments to make about the strike of the bronco busters. Said one Boston paper: "All the world champion bronco busters in Colonel W. T. Johnson's rodeo at the Boston Gardens joined the labor movement last night, declared 'a strike, won it and announced they would go back to work in tonight's show."

Said another: "Engaging in the first big strike in the long history of rodeo, sixty-one cowboys — every one a top hand and every one famous wherever broncs and wild steers are turned out of corrals — watched Col. W. T. Johnson's opening contest from the stands in Boston Gardens last night and got paid for it."

Back home, a writer in the *Calgary Herald* of June 12, 1937, commented on the strike and wondered: "Is rodeo going revolutionary? Instead of the free and easy men who follow the lure of every trail that promises bucking horses and wild steers for the wrangling, are we to have a group arguing for advantages long ignored? . . . Have we passed the time when cowboys will want to present a swift-moving pageant of riding and roping for their own amusement and that of any onlookers who happen by?"

The writer concluded that the old free days were indeed passing and that it was time the rodeo rider had a fair shake. "Some of the largest crowds gather in places where the day money is far too small. These men, travelling distances from place to place, have heavy expenses, run big risks, and take chances on returns. The sum of a season's earnings for a man in the money looks far from generous when everything has been met. It had taken the man with the saddle and chaps a long time to discover that, if a remedy is to be found, he is the one to find it. And for this reason we have the newly-formed cowboy union which has been humorously styled, the Cowboy Turtle Association."

In the same interview, Herman Linder agreed. "Cowboys must pull together just like any other group in work and play," he said, "and further, why should they not stage a strike if no other way of a proper settlement offers?"

Looking back on those days now, Herman sees the strike as the turning point for the rodeo cowboy. "That was the nucleus of the cowboy organizations right there," he said, "and we called ourselves 'The Turtles' because the turtle is slow to start but sure to get there in the end."

From that early beginning the American cowboys' movement grew and became the Rodeo Cowboys' Association, or R.C.A. of today. Quite a few years later, a man named Don Thompson of Black Diamond, Alberta, started a Canadian group and called it the Cowboys' Protective Association, which evolved into today's Canadian Rodeo Cowboys' Association or C.R.C.A. as we call it.

When the C.R.C.A. was started, Herman was on the other side of the fence. He had become a rodeo manager. But he was the Cowboy Turtles, first Vice-President and is today a life member of the R.C.A. as well as the C.R.C.A.

"We did have quite a battle with management for a while," Herman admitted. "They thought we should have no say in things at all and they tried going amateur for a while. But that didn't work. The crowd wanted to see professional riders, so management finally accepted the Association."

Next year, at their first annual meeting in Fort Worth, Texas, the Cowboy Turtles elected the executive whose names appeared on the first Turtle stationery. They were: Everett Bowman, president; Herman Linder, first vice-president; Rusty McGinty, second vice-president; and Hugh Bennett, secretary-treasurer. Event representatives were: Hughie Long, Bareback Riding; Everett Shaw, Calf Roping; Harry Knight, Saddle Bronc Riding; Dick Truitt, Steer Wrestling; and Eddie Curtis, Bull Riding.

"And the organization sure helped the cowboys tremendously," said Herman. "The young boys today have no idea what they've got to help them in competition compared to what we had. For instance, in those early days we had ten rodeo chutes at Madison Square Garden and each saddle had a number on it. If your horse was in Chute No. 5, you rode the saddle marked No. 5. And it was the same with the bareback rigging. If your horse was in Chute No. 1, you had to take the rigging marked No. 1. In those days, you might go to New York and never ride the same saddle twice!"

The year of the Cowboy Turtles' first annual meeting also marked Herman's first venture into the rodeo circuits of the American Deep South.

"Pete Knight had told me you couldn't win in the south until you had been going there for three years or so — enough time for folks to get to know you," Herman said. "I couldn't afford to go down there and work for three years for nothing like some of them could.

"But by 1937 I figured I had made a bit of a name for myself so I decided to try my hand in the Southwest. I went to Tucson, Arizona, and I won some day money there. Next, I went to Phoenix and won second in the average, and then on to a little rodeo at a place called Wickenburg, where I won. That encouraged me so much I hit San Angelo and Fort Worth, Texas, where I picked up a little day money and was fourth in the standings there."

The usual pattern for riders on the rodeo circuit was to spend the winters in these places and then head for California in the spring. But Herman didn't do that. Come spring, he headed north for home because there were calving chores to do and crops that had to be seeded.

"In 1937, I shook hands with my friend Pete Knight in Fort Worth," Herman said. "He was heading for California, as usual, and asked me if I was coming along. I told him I had work to do back home and that I'd be seeing him later on in the summer, which of course, I never did. I was only home about three weeks when word came that

Pete had been killed by a bronc named Duster at
Hayward, California. It was a big blow to all of us. He was
one of the best competitors rodeo has ever seen."

Later on that same year, Herman was destined to meet
another old friend for the last time, the bucking horse
Pardner, now called Schoolboy Rowe. It happened in 1937
at the Boston Gardens where a lot of things seemed to
happen which affected Herman and his rodeo career.
When he picked his finals horse out of the hat and saw he
had drawn Schoolboy Rowe, Herman had mixed feelings
about it. After all, this was the final event so there was a lot
of money at stake. And this horse had always managed to
dump him.

Nobody could tell how Pardner felt about it. Like
Herman, the horse had also come a long long way since
those happy days on the farm together. Ads for the big
show coming up at Madison Square Garden proclaimed
the big gelding as one of the twelve top bucking horses in
the United States. Schoolboy Rowe stood second to the
head of a list of broncs that would make the tailbone of
many a veteran rider tingle just to read it. Herman had
agreed to sell him for $250 — now he couldn't be bought
for $3,000.

As Herman strode to the chutes that afternoon, he felt
a sense of rising excitement. This was the way it should be,
he told himself. After all, a lot of the success he had
enjoyed was due to the lessons he had learned on old
Pardner. It was only right the horse should have a crack at
him again.

When he got to Chute No. 6, where Pardner was
saddled and ready, Herman spoke softly to the horse and
gave the sleek neck a couple of pats, then he climbed up
and straddled the chute, all set to lower himself into the
saddle.

"I can give you a few tips on how this old outlaw
bucks," the gateman said to Linder. "I travel with this
outfit, so I know them all."

"Thanks anyway, son," Herman grinned, "but this old
fella and I don't need any introduction. I used to own him

and he has bucked me off more times than I'd care to mention. You might say we started in rodeo together."

Then the loudspeaker was blaring his name: "Herman Linder out of Chute No. 6 on the Mighty Schoolboy Rowe!" The announcer told the crowd about Herman's string of victories in rodeos all over the States and Canada. Then he told of Schoolboy Rowe's great record — how he had only been mastered three times in the past three weeks of competition. "This is a contest between champions!" he shouted, not knowing it was also a contest between old friends.

"You ready, Herman?" he asked finally.

"Ready as I'll ever be," Herman nodded, "turn him loose!"

The erstwhile Pardner came charging out of the chutes as if it were old home week, which of course it was. He jumped and turned, jumped and turned, around and around, grunting and squealing in the old familiar way. Down came his head and up went his hind legs and he was off across the arena in a shower of dirt clods. But Herman was still with him.

"It felt as if a ton of dynamite had exploded under me," he laughed, as he recalled that ride. "There was a bit of psychology working against me too. Old Pardner had bucked me off so many times I sort of expected it to happen. I even caught myself looking for a soft spot to land. Then I took hold of myself and vowed I was going to ride the old son of a gun all the way. Just once I was going to show him who was boss!"

The crowd went wild. Even the announcer got excited. "I don't known who's trying hardest out here, the rider or the horse. But let's give them both a big hand!" he bellowed.

Amid the thunder of applause, the horn sounded and a pick-up man pounded up and picked Herman off. Linder stood watching, a little sadly, as another rider ran old Pardner away. That was the last time he ever saw the horse that had almost ended his career before it got started.

"One bucking horse is pretty much like another to me," said Herman. "You name them, and I've ridden most of them at one time or another: Bay Dynamite, Whiskey Roan, Yellow Fever, C Cross Gray, C Cross Black, Grizzly Sal, Hot Shot, Easy Money, Horn Toad, 27 Bay, Blue Dog, Slim Sweetie, Jack Dempsey, Lonely Valley Gray, High Pockets, Sweet Annie and many others. But Pardner, well, he was something special!"

CHAPTER TWELVE

MISTER RODEO

Herman Linder ended his competition riding as he had begun it — with a big win. From that first official win on Yellow Fever when he was a kid of sixteen and his first entry into big-time rodeo competition in 1929 when he won both the Canadian Saddle Bronc and Bareback titles, flowed a solid decade of spectacular triumphs. His last competition ride was made at Lewiston, Idaho, in the summer of 1939 on a reride mount named Big Enough. But the bronc wasn't big enough to toss the "Cowboy Supreme of the Western World", as one newspaper called him.

Herman began talking of retirement in 1938, but nobody would take him seriously — not even when he bet a fellow rider a case of whiskey he would ride only one more year.

"When I went back to New York that year, I talked to Everett Coleburn," said Herman. "He was one of the head guys at the Madison Square Rodeo because he was arena director at that time. He also had a share of the stock contracting. I told him I'd like to come back to New York next year and judge the rodeo there as a sort of climax to my rodeo career. He advised me to go and have a talk with Colonel Kilpatrick of the Madison Square Garden Corporation. I went up to this big fancy office and talked to the Colonel and told him what I wanted to do.

"He suggested I was too young to quit riding. But I said I was thirty-one years old and the next year I would be thirty-two, and I thought in any sport when you hit thirty-two you generally started to go down.

"And I explained how I wanted to go back home and build up my cattle ranch and start constructing a new house. He finally agreed it was probably the smart thing to do — quit while I was on top — and he gave me a contract to come back to New York in 1939 and judge the rodeo. To me, that would put the frosting on my whole career. It would be the ultimate for any cowboy that ever rode a bronc!"

The next year, Herman rode the rodeo circuit all summer, finally making that last ride in Lewiston, Idaho, and winning it. A lot of his rider friends were still unconvinced he really meant to quit, so he began taking bets again — this time at ten dollars a throw. He collected on all of them, but not without a bit of personal anguish. Quitting was a lot harder on him than he ever imagined it would be, Herman now admits.

"I subscribed to a rodeo magazine, *Hoof and Horns,* published in Tucson, Arizona, by a fine old lady we called 'Ma Hopkins'," he said. "After I'd been home for about a month, I was almost afraid to look at it. There were all my friends winning at Denver and Tucson and other places. By golly, you know, it finally struck me that after ten years of steady riding on the rodeo circuit, my friends were all on the road!

If I hadn't made those bets and told Colonel Kilpatrick I was quitting, and if I hadn't been interviewed for an article for the *Calgary Herald* that told all about my retirement, you know, I think I would've gone back. That first winter, I just about wore the living room rug out pacing up and down. I don't think if you were on dope it would be any harder to just up and quit like that. I just about went crazy. You know, I thought there'd be nothing to it, but quitting rodeo was the hardest thing I ever did in my life!"

His feelings were aggravated by his continued contact with the sport. The following year (1940), he went to the Rodeo Convention and made a deal with Leo Cremer to scout for bucking horses in Canada to use in the U.S. shows. "I worked with him for several years," said Herman, "and then I started buying for the Lightning C Ranch, which was Gene Autry's outfit."

"That took him away a lot," Mrs. Linder added, "but by that time our son, George, and our daughter, Rose Marie, were born, so I stayed home. It's no fun travelling with a family, especially in the heat of summer."

It was during this in-between period in 1943, while he was on his way to judge the rodeo at Cheyenne, Wyoming, that Herman heard the news of his father's death. The older Linder had fallen while helping stack hay back home on the farm.

Herman got into the rodeo promotion and management end of it more by chance than by design. He had been on the committee of the local rodeo in Cardston for several years and had done a lot to streamline the show so that it functioned more smoothly. When the Fort Macleod Stampede people came over and saw how well the Cardston Rodeo was going they asked Herman to run theirs too. Other towns and cities followed suit. When asked for advice, Calgary Stampede officials would unanimously recommend Herman Linder.

Herman soon found himself operating rodeos in Coleman, High River, Lethbridge and Medicine Hat, and in several places in neighboring British Columbia. As his fame spread as a rodeo manager, he was invited to stage a rodeo in Vancouver. Here, his fame can better be described as notoriety because the show folded after a short run for reasons peculiar to Vancouver, although London, England, offered the same obstacles to a lesser degree. But he bounced right back by building up the Edmonton Rodeo until it is one of the bigger ones in the country today. Then came the climax in 1967 when he was asked to put on the big Western Show at Expo in Montreal.

"Some of the most memorable times in my rodeo manager's career, though, came in the smaller places," Herman recalled. "Take the Medicine Hat show now, it was a big success right from the start. I began by providing stock for this rodeo and ended up managing it for twenty-odd years. One of the most amusing shows I ever staged happened in Lethbridge during the Second World War. The fairs and everything had been closed down for a few years, then the Kinsmen's Club and I got together and decided to put on a rodeo and get things started again right while the War was on. The fellas in the Club and I were all about the same age — in our mid to late-thirties. This is an age when a fella can't afford to lose, that's for sure, and we were just about all in the same boat as far as finances went.

"One particular incident I will never forget came when it had been raining off and on all the week before we were scheduled to open," Herman chuckled, "and it also rained heavily the last night before the show. Doc Kearns of Lethbridge was Club president at that time and we were in the Marquis Hotel worrying about what the weather was going to do to us. Every once in a while we'd step out on the fire escape outside our window and look at the sky. The rain kept pouring down and that old sky was so black you couldn't see a thing.

"In spite of the seriousness of the situation — we were to have a big parade too in the morning to start things off — I couldn't help but laugh. There was Doc Kearns with a worried look on his face, chewing furiously on a stick of gum like a baseball pitcher on the mound. 'We're sunk,' he groaned, 'we're sunk. You know, I wouldn't mind if I wasn't Kinsmen president right now.'

"Well sir," said Herman, "When we got up next morning around five or six o'clock, it had quit raining. But everything looked soaked right through and the sky was still glowering like it might start raining again at any moment. I went out to the grounds before the parade started to have a look at things. There I found one of the Kinsmen members hard at work with a team of horses hitched to a small stone boat, out in the center of the arena where a sort of lake had formed with a few feet of water in it. That stone boat had a fifty-gallon barrel on it, and there he was, dipping away with a pail, trying to drain that lake. I realize those Club members were determined to do everything they could to help, but where he ever got the idea he could bail out that lake like a rowboat, I'll never know. I wish I had a movie of it."

But the big parade did go on as planned and the Kinsmen had a riding troop all decked out in woolly chaps. Then, just as the parade came to an end, the sun came bursting out. The clouds rapidly disappeared until there wasn't one to be found in the whole sky. Herman and the Club members breathed a mighty sigh of relief.

"Anyway, our rodeo went on at two o'clock as scheduled and we had a terrific crowd," said Herman. "There was a fella there named Blair Holland, who did some bareback riding and was also our announcer. When it came his turn to ride in the bareback contest, he drew a horse that just took off at a run for our 'lake' in the middle of the arena. Reaching the water's edge, the horse came to an abrupt stop and turned, and Blair went sailing off into the water. He just stood there, sort of dazed, up to his neck in the stuff and the people roared. It was the hit of the show!

"Actually, with that lake out there, quite a few contestants took a ducking. The crowd just brought the house down with their yelling. In spite of the fact the arena surface was all muddy, nobody seemed to mind a bit — except maybe the riders.

"It ended up with the Kinsmen and myself and a partner making a bit of profit. The Club got $1,000. and my partner and I split $1,000 You know, I'm sure if somebody had come to us the night before, when we were so worried about the weather, and said, 'Now boys, we'll take all the gamble out of the show for you. If you fellas will just go ahead with the rodeo, we'll handle all expenses and even give you a little money to boot,' I'm sure we would've signed off right there and then.

"That was one of the most amusing rodeos I ever put on: in fact, after having things turn out so well, the Kinsmen and I ran a rodeo there for several years until the war ended. Then the Lethbridge Exhibition people started their fair up again and took the show away from us."

But Fort Macleod elected to leave its rodeo show in the able hands of the veteran Cardston rider. Many years later, that history-conscious town paid tribute to yet another veteran by naming its spanking new rodeo grounds after him. The grounds became Midnight Stadium in honor of Midnight, perhaps the most famous bucking horse of them all.

"He gave no quarter and asked for none," says part of the inscription on a plaque that was unveiled at the Stadium. The unveiling was done by Jim McNab, Midnight's original owner. The horse's career started when he threw an Indian cowboy who had mounted him to ride to the chuck wagon for dinner during a roundup on the nearby Blood Reserve.

Midnight made his first appearance at the Calgary Stampede in 1924. After tossing every cowboy who was unlucky enough to draw him, the horse's fame soon spread. He was finally bought by "Strawberry Red" Woll and Pete Welch of the Alberta Stampede Company Ltd., for $500. Midnight's bucking career progressed until he was retired in 1933 at the end of the Frontier Days show in Cheyenne, Wyoming. After many appearances at various rodeos for the next three years, he died at one of them — the Denver Show — in 1936. A full funeral was held for the old trouper and his remains were buried at Colorado Ranch. Later, the remains were exhumed and removed to the Cowboys Hall of Fame at Oklahoma City.

Herman Linder, who had helped take care of Midnight on the trip to England, has been honored at a few halls of fame too. There was the time back in his riding days when he was nominated "Man of the Year" by that same Oklahoma City National Hall of Fame. In the Horseman's Hall of Fame at Calgary, his figure has been cast, life-size, along with those of three other cowboy greats who have made outstanding contributions to the Calgary Stampede down the years: Pete Knight, Clem Gardner — the first cowboy champion — Dick Cosgrave, chuck wagon driver and longtime arena director.

Lethbridge has also honored him. Said writer Ron Watmough in one Alberta paper: "The greatest cowboy, Herman Linder, has been named to the Lethbridge and District Exhibition's Hall of Fame. Linder, who has ridden wild horses further straight up and down than the average man drives his car in a year, was cited last year as the eleventh person to receive the honor. As a rodeo manager, Herman ... helped the rodeo game grow from small community entertainment to a 700-shows-a-year business on this continent."

By this time, papers all over the country were calling Herman Linder "Canada's Mister Rodeo". Then came the Vancouver fiasco.

CHAPTER THIRTEEN

THE GREAT VANCOUVER HULLABALOO

People who know Herman Linder agree he is both a gentleman and a gentle man. You would have about as much chance of hanging a Cruelty to Animals charge on him and making it stick as you would have making a similar charge against St. Francis of Assisi.

Nevertheless, such a charge was diligently pursued against Herman in Vancouver, B.C. in 1949 and was maintained through two courts over a period of a year until the Supreme Court of B.C. finally did what should have been done in the first place — they examined the case on the basis of facts rather than emotion, and threw it out.

The charge against Herman was pushed by certain elements within the Vancouver branch of the S.P.C.A. who thought they saw a chance to keep rodeo out of Vancouver. When a bronc was found with some wounds high on its neck they claimed these were made by spurs and laid the cruelty charge. This was found to be untrue, so they said the calf roping was cruel. After that, they attacked the bucking strap. Fortunately, pollution wasn't a big thing in those days, or they might have got him on polluting the arena with horse manure.

They weren't really after Herman at all: they were after rodeo itself. Rodeo was not to be allowed to contaminate the hearts and minds of the citizens of Vancouver, like it had the citizens of every other city and town in North America. Vancouver was to remain pure and free, and they succeeded. Although the charges against Herman were dropped, so was rodeo as far as Vancouver was concerned. The sponsors of the show decided they'd had enough adverse publicity to last them a lifetime and gave up on the idea. Rodeo never did make a successful comeback in the coast city after that.

It all started when the Rotary Club of Marpole — a district in south Vancouver — decided the citizens of Vancouver should get a chance to see a real, live rodeo show, just like their more fortunate fellows in other parts of the Continent. The place chosen for the event was Callister Park, which is located just west of the city's main Exhibition Grounds at Hastings Park.

The rodeo was to last from May 24th to May 28th, and one newspaper hailed it as the "Biggest rodeo Vancouver has ever seen." Another paper called it the "Sixth largest rodeo on the Continent." There were all the well-known cowboy events, clowns, Slim Pickins and his famous bull-fighting act and a girls' drill team from Seattle. The Rotary Club's rodeo committee, which was headed by Nat Bailey — famous for his White Spot restaurants — was confident this would be the biggest and best stampede ever to come to Vancouver.

It was certainly the most highly publicized. The show began with a near riot because of a misunderstanding about the tickets. Many people failed to read the instructions on stubs bought from street and store vendors which read: "Please exchange stubs for reserve seats by mailing, or presenting same to Hick's ticket bureau, 610 Dunsmuir Street."

Thousands of eager fans had to be turned away after waiting in line for as long as two hours because there was not enough space to handle them. While about 8,000 people jammed the seats inside, another 10,000 stood outside demanding to get in. Several scuffles broke out in the two-block-long lineup the first afternoon. Headlines screamed: "Huge Crowd Misses Stampede" and "Ten Thousand Irate as Doors Shut."

But the real trouble was brewing inside where an S.P.C.A. inspector had found one of the broncs, Rimrock, had some wounds on its neck. He reported it to his superiors, and Herman was hauled into the Police Magistrate's Court. Here, Vancouver S.P.C.A. secretary-manager David Ricardo testified that he saw five marks on Rimrock's left shoulder "oozing fresh blood" as the bronc left the arena on May 24th, after a ride. Rimrock had come right out of the chutes bucking with the rider raking from shoulder to flank with the spurs, he said, and a bucking strap was tight under the horse's rear lower belly to make him buck more. He said he had examined the bronc in the corral later with a part-time S.P.C.A. inspector named James Payne, and had seen the wounds. He also testified that a calf had been thrown to the ground so roughly in the calf roping contest the animal was stunned.

Rodeo buffs know a rider has to work his spurs fore and aft or he will lose points. They also know if a rider raked high enough to cause such marks on a horse's neck he would lose his balance and fall off. Later, a veterinarian testified the marks on Rimrock were definitely not spur marks.

Herman received the summons that Saturday night, saying he was to appear in court the next Monday. Charged with him were two American cowboys, who left town before their summonses could be served. This left Herman to face the charge alone. As he didn't even know what animals were involved in the dispute, he asked for time and the case was adjourned until the following Thursday.

When the trial finally opened on that day, the S.P.C.A. claimed Rimrock was so seriously injured by the rider's spurs he had to be withdrawn from the contest. Nobody pointed out that, once ridden, a bronc is withdrawn for that Go Round, and another takes its place. At eight seconds or less per ride, bucking horses are used only a few minutes in an entire season.

Rimrock's owner, stock contractor Harold Ring of Wilbur, Washington, denied the bronc had received any spur wounds, insisting Rimrock had been bitten by another horse while en route to Vancouver. This was later found to be true when a veterinarian at the Border confirmed the bronc had the marks on him when he entered Canada. A little investigation before the fact would have revealed this, and preempted the case.

In the meantime, old Rimrock was prancing around Callister Park like a two-year-old, oblivious to the storm being built around him by misguided animal lovers. Unlike his "defenders", Rimrock knew bucking horses actually lived the life of Riley. As only one horse in a thousand makes a good bucker, such horses are pampered. The average age of all broncs in professional rodeo is fifteen to twenty-five years and every major string of buckers has at least one past the age of twenty. In the horse world, this is a ripe old age.

They are also protected from maltreatment by a set of rules produced by the Canadian Rodeo Cowboys Association in conjunction with the national S.P.C.A. But a lot of people don't know this and they may react out of emotion rather than knowledge and reason. Some buckers love to buck and do the best they can to unseat their riders, just like a thoroughbred strives to win at the race track.

Old Pardner was a prime example of a natural bucker, who often bucked without benefit of a flanker. After he had pridefully done his job, he used to sniff around for the oats he had been led to believe were his due — not exactly the actions of a terrified animal.

At the hearing, a great thing was made of the fact spurs were used. But, as an onlooker pointed out, even the Vancouver Police use spurs. "Spurs, spurs, spurs, that's all they talked about," he said. "The R.C.M.P. use spurs, the Vancouver Police use spurs, every cowboy uses spurs. If they didn't, the horses wouldn't respond."

But Police Court magistrate W. B. McInnes didn't see it that way. Herman was fined $100 or thirty days in jail. The decision was appealed but the case wasn't heard until the following January. Flushed with victory, the S.P.C.A. board met to discuss rodeos in general and how to stop them.

"You know, those marks on Rimrock were just little marks," Herman said, recalling the event. "With a gray horse they show up badly. If he'd been a dark horse nobody would have seen them.

"One of the S.P.C.A. inspectors was a retired veterinarian," he explained, "and when they asked him if a calf was knocked out during the throwing, he said yes. Then they asked him if it was hurt, or seemed to be injured. He said no, so that part of the charge was thrown out. You know, the S.P.C.A. wouldn't let this retired vet testify any more after that."

"Actually, those inspectors were real nice guys," he added. "They weren't out to raise the roof, or anything. They only brought it up in the first place to show they were on the job. But the whole thing got out of hand. That Friday night the press came out with a story that crucified rodeo. There was a writer named Jack Scott who said, if rodeo was considered to be a sport, it's time we started to think about the kind of sports we had.

"Then the inspectors felt they had to try and do something to counteract this bad publicity, or they'd be out of a job. They were extra men working for wages, you see. Every time we went into court the head inspector would come over and shake hands with me and say, 'Now, this is not a personal thing.'"

Here is what *Vancouver Sun* writer Jack Scott had to say in a write-up that must have wrung tears from the lions which guard the entrance to Vancouver's Court House: "Pleasure from torment is the inescapable appeal to the passions that are calculatingly aroused by the rodeo. It offers a respectable respite from those considerations of kindliness, pity and mercy that have kept the human spirit from the pit, and so it becomes one more negation of the basic ideals and hopes of civilization. That is why I choose to step into the uncrowded ranks of those who will take the time to put their objection on the record."

As might be expected, this caused a spate of letters to the editor condemning the Marpole Rotary Club for bringing such a disgusting spectacle to their fair city.

Said one: "The Rotary Club of Marpole is guilty of the most dishonorable thing of its career in bringing rodeo to Vancouver under its sponsorship. If there is anything on the face of the Earth that is cruel and devilish, it's a rodeo."

Said another: "Surely it is a step backward instead of forward for Vancouver when a well-known service club resorts to such means as a rodeo to provide funds for a community center . . . it's a very low form of entertainment — rough, coarse and useless."

From the *Vancouver News Herald*: "I wonder how many stampede fans have seen the carcass of an animal after it has been in the rodeo arena for a few days? It is not a happy sight."

This was really reaching for it. The dictionary defines "carcass" as the "dead body of an animal or human." And of course rodeo animals don't stay in arenas for days, only a few seconds a few times a week.

But there were some press people who came to the defence of both the Marpole Rotary and rodeo. Writing in the *Vancouver Province,* Jean Howarth observed: "I notice Marpole Rotarians have been getting quite a dusting up from various sources for daring to hold a rodeo in Vancouver. Having been brought up on the Calgary Stampede, I don't naturally see eye-to-eye with these critics. Their chief complaint is that rodeo permits cruelty to animals. And, although I watched rodeo day in and day out for thirteen Stampedes, I don't think I ever saw any deliberate cruelty to animals. Unless you would call a cowboy an animal."

Alderman R. K. Gervin told the Vancouver City Council he saw the rodeo and didn't think it was cruel. He figured the horses and the calves enjoyed it more than anybody, said one news report.

A woman wrote in to one of the leading dailies to say: "These hypocrites that are howling about cruelty to animals don't hesitate to wear their fur coats, nor bother much about the cruelty of traps that trap these animals — real cruelty to animals. But they don't see that or they'd close their mouths when they wear fur coats."

In the meantime, the cowboys continued to take their usual amount of body punishment and nobody charged anybody on that score. Such headlines as: "Three Cowboys Hurt at Night Show" and "Brahma Bulls Bounce Unlucky Cowboys," appeared daily. A cartoon showed nine S.P.C.A. inspectors grouped around a very fit-looking horse and ignoring a pitifully beat-up cowboy lying on the ground.

Great headlines slashed across the front pages over a period of several months: "Rodeo Manager Fined: City Magistrate Denounces Rodeo!" "Rodeo Cruelty Conviction Quashed!" Never did a rodeo show, or any show for that matter, get so much free publicity. The sad part was that Herman's show was not able to cash in on it.

The appeal hearing came up before Judge J. C. Lennox in County Court in January of the following year. All the main actors of the drama were on hand, even Rimrock, who got a free trip to Canada, although it's doubtful if he appreciated the honor as the weather left much to be desired. A headline made much of the fact Judge Lennox had to push through slush to get to the hearing.

While Rimrock cooled his heels in a truck outside the court wondering what it was all about, an argument was going on as to whether the court should move outside to have a look at the bronc or whether the bronc should be brought inside to have a look at the court.

Lawyer Henry Castillou, who was acting for Herman, felt the court had to have a look at the horse, one way or another, so he could prove the neck marks had not been made by spurs.

"I would like you to have a look at this horse," he told Judge Lennox.

"He's right outside the building now," owner Harold Ring added.

"Has he got a parking meter?" the Judge quipped.

Crown Prosecutor Stewart McMorran, who was fighting the appeal on behalf of the Crown, objected.

"I am opposed to any such viewing," he said. "It is my understanding that in any case where a summary conviction is being appealed, the court may not leave the place of sitting."

Judge Lennox cut in here to say the consent of both counsels might be necessary in order to view the horse.

"Does my learned friend refuse to allow a viewing?" defence lawyer Castillou asked the Prosecutor.

"I am not protesting to contest a view," said McMorran, "only that it is not proper for the court to leave the place of sitting."

"Then I will have to bring the horse into court," Castillou said.

"It seems so," the Judge observed.

"I don't see why we cannot," Castillou nodded.

"Well, I don't mind," Judge Lennox said, "but I don't think a demonstration is necessary."

It was agreed Rimrock would remain outside. Instead, officials from the Border crossing station at Blaine were called in to testify they actually had a record to show the horse was injured in the neck before coming into Canada. In addition, Dr. Gordon C. McDonald — a Lulu Island veterinary surgeon — testified that scab marks on the left rear part of Rimrock's shoulder resembled marks made by teeth. He did not agree with the Crown Prosecutor that the scabs were caused by spurring. Dr. McDonald said he had examined the horse on the thirtieth and said the wounds were probably inflicted eight or ten days before. Herman was acquitted on the Rimrock charge and also on the charge of cruelty to a calf, and he thought he was well in the clear. But the court had other plans.

Next thing Herman knew he was defending himself against a charge of using a bucking strap, or flanker, on a horse to make it buck. This was the same type of sheepskin-lined flank strap he had brought back from Australia years earlier. It was approved by S.P.C.A. branches and Humane Societies for use in rodeos all over the North American continent, but they'd never seen one in Vancouver.

Said a write-up in the *Vancouver Province* of January 25th, 1950: "Rodeo promoter Herman Linder all but saddled himself in Appeal Court today in an attempt to show that the flank strap used on horses at the Rotary Stampede last May could not cause injury. Mr. Linder, who has himself won honors in four countries, was appealing a Police Court ruling on abuse of an animal. His detailed description of rodeo techniques supported similar evidence given Monday by Harold Ring of Wilbur, Washington, who had engaged in some heated word battles with Assistant City Prosecutor, Stewart McMorran, who maintained spurs and harness used in bronco busting contests were painful goads."

On February 3, 1950, Judge Lennox brought down his decision. He ruled that flank straps do constitute unnecessary abuse of a horse, and dismissed Herman's appeal from his previous conviction on a cruelty charge. Herman was stunned at the decision and so was the whole world of rodeo. This posed a threat to a multi-million-dollar industry. Now Herman had plenty of friends to back him when he took the case to the Appelate Division of the Supreme Court of British Columbia.

"By this time we had had enough," said Herman, looking back on these incredible events. "A ruling like that could not be allowed to go unchallenged. It wasn't just my fight now. It was an attack against the whole rodeo industry."

Herman got in touch with Pinky Baylen of Pendleton, Oregon who was president of the International Rodeo Association, and Baylen assured him he would help in the fight. It was no problem getting the Canadian Stampede

Managers Association to back his cause because Herman
was the current president of that group. For good measure,
the Cowboys Protective Association, the Calgary Stampede, and the Rodeo Cowboys Association also joined the
fray. All contributed money to the defence.

In the meantime, Herman's lawyer, Henry Castillou,
had been made a County Court judge, so lawyer John L.
Farris was engaged to take the case to the Court of Appeal.
After careful deliberation, the three appeal judges, headed
by Mr. Justice C. H. O'Halloran, reversed the original
decisions and both Herman and rodeo were vindicated.
The prosecution was left without a leg to stand on.

If a flank strap was a restraint on a horse, so was a
saddle cinch the Appeal Court pointed out. Did the
prosecution figure all saddle horses should be banned
too?

But the guys in the black hats had the last laugh. It was
April before the Supreme Court made this ruling and too
late for the Marpole Rotary Club to get tickets printed and
book space at Callister Park. Plans for the rodeo were
cancelled for that year.

"We are very happy about the decision upholding Mr.
Linder," said club president, Jack Diamond, "But we want
topnotch cowboys for our show and most of those men are
solidly booked now for this year. We will probably have a
show next year, and if things work out it will probably turn
into an annual event."

The Rotary Club never did have another rodeo.
Members were afraid of the adverse publicity they might
get, and Vancouver's chance to see a real live Western
show rode off into the sunset.

"If we had won the first appeal, as we should have,
next year's rodeo would've gone on as planned," Herman
maintains. "And it would have been a real success because
the whole city — in fact, the whole of Canada — was
talking about the case. Every time we came to court the
place was jammed full. Never did we have such publicity!
It was the only rodeo I've ever been to in my life where we

had to turn thousands of people away. Inside the park, they were hanging from the rafters!"

It was ten years before anybody in Vancouver got up enough nerve to attempt another rodeo. This time, it was the powerful Pacific National Exhibition, a much more formidable opponent than the Marpole Rotary Club. And who did they engage to stage this rodeo? Why, none other than the very best producer in the business, Herman Linder of Cardston, Alberta. Nothing was too good for the citizens of Vancouver!

World Champion bronco buster, Casey Tibbs, drolly noted this event in a column he wrote called "Let 'Er Buck." Said Tibbs: "Ten years have gone by and at last Herman is producing another rodeo in Vancouver. This time at the Pacific National Exhibition. The S.P.C.A. made more noise this time than they did before. They publicly asked people not to attend. Said rodeo was inhumane and unkind to dumb animals. And besides that, August when the rodeo is to be held is the busiest season for the S.P.C.A. They said if the rodeo went on they would have to hire extra help because at that time of year they usually have to kill about 2,000 head of cats."

The S.P.C.A. *did* urge the people to stay away from the rodeo so as to make it a financial failure, but not all agreed with this. Patrick Burns told a meeting of the Vancouver branch that the Society has no business trying to keep rodeos out of Vancouver, that it should be concerned only with preventing cruelty to animals, as its name implied. Burns also predicted the publicity caused by the S.P.C.A.'s fight against rodeo would attract about 25,000 more people to the P.N.E. event that year.

The papers made quite a thing out of the cat story and Herman did what he could to help. He called them and had them send out reporters and photographers to see his fourteen cats. Herman loves cats and keeps a cow to supply them with milk, the stories said.

"When my cats have kittens, I go out of my way to find homes for them," he told reporters. "I certainly wouldn't think of destroying them."

Tom Hughes, an S.P.C.A. director, said the Society would need to hire nine extra inspectors if the P.N.E. went ahead with its plans to stage a rodeo. This was police work they were doing, he said, and the police should pay the extra cost.

And of course the *Vancouver Sun's* Jack Scott took off after the cowboys again in an especially determined way. The zealous columnist said: "Please put my name down to go all the way with those gentle people who will be opposing, however fruitlessly, the decision to include a rodeo as a regular attraction at our Pacific National Exhibition ... My own resolve to oppose this popular form of sadism is linked directly to the experience of taking my kids to a rodeo. That was ten years ago, but the memory of their reaction and their simple, uncomplicated disgust at a spectacle which relies on an animal's fear and torment for the amusement of the mob, left me with the conviction that no amount of rationalizing can justify it."

Scott then went on to say it was nonsense to say rodeo represents courage and skills used normally on the range. He once visited Joe Bews's ranch in the foothills west of High River, Alberta, and there was a big difference between ranch functions and the "contrived brutality" of the rodeo arena, he said.

Ironically, in 1971 Joe Bews's son, Tom, was named Canadian Champion All Around Cowboy, and was top man in both the saddle bronc and steer wrestling. Tom broke into the top five of the saddle bronc competitors in 1964, says the *Canadian Rodeo News,* and has been out of that select circle just once. In 1972, he placed twenty-two times in the saddle bronc event, winning four of them outright. He is married to Rose Marie Linder, the daughter of gentle Herman Linder.

In his column "Good Morning", writer Wilf Bennet talks about people who go overboard and become fanatically attached to animals and animal causes, mostly through a misunderstanding. Bennet, a longtime observer and reporter of rodeos, says their cruelty has been almost hysterically exaggerated. He observed sadly that he was receiving Olympian frowns from colleague Jack Scott for his support of rodeo.

Said Herman Linder in a letter to Bennet before the P.N.E. show: "We who produce rodeos are no more inclined to treat our animals poorly than are you to see this done. Who thinks more highly of his four-legged friend than the man whose livelihood depends on that animal. Rodeo is a part of North American heritage. It exists only because the cowboys more than any other horse trainer in history, gave the horse an even break. The cowboy on a bucking horse has become a symbol — almost a trademark — of a whole era in American history.

"Today, it is a contest that plays to over fifteen million people a year. It is regulated and administered by the Rodeo Cowboys Association in the United States and the Canadian Rodeo Cowboys Association in Canada. Rules and regulations are strictly enforced. Together with the S.P.C.A. and the American Humane Society, they have developed a standard set of regulations that safeguard rodeo stock from abuse. While rodeo action is always violent, it is not dangerous or brutal to animals. You have my pledge that the P.N.E. Rodeo will be carefully conducted under these regulations."

The P.N.E. predicted its rodeo would be a real rival for the Calgary Stampede and that the West Coast show would become an annual event. As things turned out, Calgary had no need to fear the loss of its laurels.

Although the public ignored the pleas of the S.P.C.A. about boycotting the show, another force stepped in to ensure that Vancouver citizens would be spared this wickedness. The name of this new menace was Jupiter Pluvius, the rainmaker. The S.P.C.A. must have been neglecting their small animals' eradication program, for it rained cats and dogs, as the saying goes.

There was also another mixup on the tickets which caused a lot of people to miss the show. Somehow people got the idea if they left the main Exhibition Grounds and crossed the road to attend the rodeo at Callister Park, they'd have to pay to get back into the big park (Hastings Park) again.

"This wasn't so," said Herman Linder. "This was spelled out in a great banner over the main gateway which said those who left for the rodeo could get in again. But people just didn't seem to see that sign. Coupled with all that rain, we lost $15,000. Then in 1969, we tried again and lost some more money," he concluded, shaking his head. "But I still think if we'd been able to go back in 1950 right after we won our case, and then kept coming back, we'd have gotten the thing going."

Vancouver is just not a rodeo town. Rodeo belongs in the land beyond the mountains, in the high, dry plains country. Well, maybe not so dry. When Herman moved his show on to Edmonton after the 1949 fiasco, he almost got rained out again. But Edmonton people have a way of getting around things like that.

CHAPTER FOURTEEN

EDMONTON TO EXPO

When it became evident there would be no chance of holding a rodeo in Vancouver in 1950, Herman had the chutes hauled to Edmonton, where he had been invited to put on a show. It was to be held at the Exhibition Grounds, just in front of the grandstand.

"Very seldom does a new business start making money right at the beginning," said Herman philosophically, "and the Edmonton Rodeo was no exception. The first year, we had to hold it outside and it was cool and rained a little. And that wasn't all, we just couldn't get any publicity. In fact, one newspaper was pretty rough on us. Not because they figured rodeo was cruel, or anything like that. They just figured Edmonton shouldn't be doing something Calgary was doing. Edmonton people like to be original, you know."

The first Edmonton Rodeo lost about $6,000. Compared to the Vancouver loss, this wasn't very much, but coming on top of the Vancouver loss it was enough to give a cowboy the seven-year itch. But Herman kept at it with the same tenacity and concentration that made him a top bronc rider. After four years of changing dates around and reshuffling the acts, it finally began to make money. Today, it is one of the biggest rodeos in Canada.

"I started it and ran it for the first ten years," Herman nodded, "and I gambled my own money on it. If the show lost money, I had to pay one third — if it made money, I got a third share of th profits. Of course, after it got going real good and made money steadily, the Exhibition took it over."

Although the show lost a little money that first year, Herman and the Exhibition Association were encouraged to try again in 1951, because the people who attended had shown so much enthusiasm. In spite of the coolness and the drizzle, they lustily cheered each event as it came.

The weatherman must have been in cahoots with the Vancouver S.P.C.A. because this time he pulled out all the stops. For the whole week before the show it poured and poured. It was like standing under Niagara Falls.

"Out in front of that grandstand it was a sea of mud," said Herman. "Sunday night, or I should say Monday morning, about three o'clock I looked out the window of my room at the downpour and I was just sick. You see, what we had lost last year would've been peanuts to what we stood to lose this time. The stock was there, the boys had come from all over the place and the acts were ready to go. I would've had to pay the stock contractor and the acts — show or no show. The advertising money was all spent. Why, we would probably have lost $20,000 to $30,000."

But Herman hadn't been called Lucky Linder for nothing. As it happened, the Edmonton Gardens — a big enclosed arena — had featured a horse show about a week before and the dirt was still on the floor. Herman knew this because he had walked through the place that afternoon. For a long while he lay in bed, wondering about the possibilities of moving his show inside. Then suddenly he reached for the phone.

"It was about six o'clock and getting a bit light, so I decided to phone Jim Paul," he said. "Jim was general manager of the Edmonton Exhibition at that time and one of the nicest fellas I ever worked with. Just a wonderful person! I asked what he thought about having us move inside, and we talked it over for a few minutes.

"Finally he said: 'Well, I'm still in bed.' I said I was too. 'Tell you what you do — you get dressed and have a bite of breakfast and I'll meet you at the arena at seven o'clock,' he told me."

Both men arrived at the arena right on the dot of seven. They walked around inside for half an hour mentally going over the problems of getting the chutes inside and where to place them. Then Linder told Paul he figured they would be able to do it in time for the show that night. Just how, he wasn't sure, but he was determined to have a mighty good crack at it.

Once they had decided to move, Jim Paul got in touch with the local radio stations. The stations cooperated by plugging the show all day, telling people the show was moving inside and that everybody should come. Herman had fourteen permanent employees, but he knew he would need a lot more hands than that so he went uptown to the hotels where the cowboys were staying and asked them if they'd give him a hand.

"By nine o'clock we had fifty cowboys down there, all raring to go," said Herman proudly. "In those days the chutes were bolted together — not all in one piece like the steel chutes of today. I imagine some of those front pieces would weigh pretty close to half a ton, but with six or seven guys to grab a hold of each piece we had no trouble loading them on the trucks."

The crews worked straight through the day, laying off only for lunch. And the work didn't even stop then because they took their lunch break in shifts. The cowboys were more anxious to see the show go on than anybody because they wouldn't otherwise get a chance at any money. By six o'clock that night — two hours before the show had to open — everything was ready to start. Outside, the rain poured steadily down and it kept raining most of that week.

"There was the odd little crack in the arena roof," said Herman, "and the water kept dripping down on us, but we had a great show. We didn't make any fortune, but we ended up with $2,000 in the black, and that was a lot better than we had expected. Now, we thought, we've really got her beat as far as Edmonton is concerned. But things didn't work out that way."

The rodeo producer's lot is not a happy one. Next year, the weather was just beautiful at Edmonton. It was so good the people poured out into the lake country west of the city and again the show lost money. Herman and the Exhibition board got together and decided they were trying to hold the show at the wrong time of the year. Herman wanted to hold it during the big March Bull Sale, but the Board didn't like this idea either. Finally they decided on April.

"From then on the show was a success," said Herman. "We started selling out on Friday and Saturday nights and had a good crowd most of each week. The Edmonton show is one of the top rodeos in Canada now, and I'm proud to have had a hand in getting it started."

Over the next fifteen years Herman Linder's name became synonymous with rodeo. With the exception of the Vancouver trouble, his shows were a big hit wherever he went. Then in 1965 to top off his great rodeo saga came an invitation to put on a rodeo at Expo 67 in Montreal.

When it came to choosing a man to stage this important rodeo, Herman Linder won hands down. In a letter to John Pratt, deputy director and producer of entertainment, Canadian Corporation for the 1967 World Exhibition, Montreal, Centennial Commissioner John Fisher had this to say: "I understand an old friend of mine, Herman Linder of Cardston, Alberta, is one of the two rodeo producers being considered for your rodeo in Expo's amphitheater. I have known Herman for many years and he is tops as far as I'm concerned in rodeo productions ... You cannot get anybody more knowledgeable. He is a real showman and I think the experts in the business would confirm this."

This was a personal plug from John Fisher, our "Mr. Canada", for a cowboy who had established his reputation over the years as Canada's "Mr. Rodeo".

Writing to Dave Dauphinee, head of the amphitheater division World Exhibition, Montreal, the late Maurice E. Hartnett, former manager of the Calgary Exhibition and Stampede, was just as emphatic as Fisher in recommending Herman for the job as manager. Said Hartnett: "Linder has a good working association with Reg Kessler who is also one of rodeo's outstanding personalities and a Canadian who has won top honors for bronc riding. Linder and Kessler, in my opinion, have access to the best rodeo stock in both the United States and Canada. Each is highly regarded for his reputation as a former contestant ... I must tell you frankly that I would not hesitate a moment in selecting Linder as your producer. In fact, I feel it would be a great mistake not to do so."

For handling the publicity for the Expo rodeo, Hartnett recommended Fred Kennedy, retired publicity director for the Calgary Stampede and also a friend of Herman Linder's. "Rodeo publicity is highly specialized, requires an encyclopedic knowledge of rodeo, its history, its people, its achievements, and its aspirations," Hartnett explained. In his opinion, having a top flight team such as Linder, Kessler, and Kennedy to put the Expo show together would be a guarantee of its success.

"You could say that Expo invitation was a climax to my career as a promoter," said Herman. "It was quite a challenge because the complete production of every phase of the rodeo was in my hands. I was responsible for setting up the chutes and corrals, helping with the advertising, contracting for the stock, and arranging for the freight and feed. I had to sign all the cheques for every dollar that was spent on the rodeo, which came pretty close to a quarter of a million dollars. But the ultimate surprise was that it actually made some money for Expo. I guess it was the first World's Fair rodeo in history to make money."

Herman contracted stock with his longtime friend and associate Reg Kessler of Rosemary, Alberta. When it came to shipping the cattle and horses east, he had his first real introduction into the weird and wonderful world of Canadian freight rates. The first thing he learned was that it would cost a lot less to ship the animals to Montreal than to ship them back to Calgary. Here, his experience in horse trading came in handy.

Months before the actual shipping date, he went to both the C.P.R. and C.N.R. to see if he could play one against the other. He'd say to one, "Now, we want to ship both ways. Unless you can give us the same freight rate coming and going I'll deal with the other fellas." Eventually, with a substantial saving, he got an agreement that the rate would be the same.

"It would be amusing if it wasn't so ridiculous," he laughed. "But you know, when we came to ship back, they were still going to charge us this extra money. I had to show them a letter from the Powers That Be saying I was to have the same rate both ways before they'd agree to it. The rate they wanted to charge for coming back was one-third more than the rate going down. As I said, it would be amusing unless you were the one who had to pay it."

But Herman Linder almost didn't make it to Expo. On July 8th, 1967 he had the worst accident of his career — long after he had quit riding broncos and insurance companies had finally decided he was as good a risk as anybody.

When it happened, Herman was serving as arena director at the Fort Macleod Stampede. He was riding around, directing activities in front of the chutes, when suddenly his horse was struck from behind by a loose bronc named Jimmy Brown, which was owned by Reg Kessler's Rodeo Stock Company. Linder had just turned his saddle horse around after watching Marty Wood of Calgary — 1966 Saddle Bronc champion — finish his ride and get hauled off safely by the pick-up man, when Jimmy Brown roared in like a runaway express train. The bronc, which had been heading normally for the catch pens at the other end of the arena, suddenly swerved and charged back to the chutes at full tilt. It plowed into Herman's saddle horse, sending horse and rider to the ground with a crash. Then the bronco added to the damage and confusion by falling on top of the prostrate horse and rider.

Cowboys hurriedly dragged the unconscious Herman out from under the tangle of kicking horses. He was rushed to Fort Macleod Hospital suffering from several fractured ribs, punctured lungs, and shock. Doctors were particularly worried that Herman might have sustained permanent damage to his lungs and for a short while he was put on the critical list. But, as before, "Lucky Linder" proved he was not only lucky but tough.

By the following Sunday, Warner Linder was telling reporters his brother was feeling pretty miserable, but that he expected to be discharged from the hospital in less than a week. He had to, Warner explained, because he had rodeos to produce for the Medicine Hat Exhibition and other Southern Alberta events, not to mention his commitment to stage the great Western show at Expo 67 in October. There was just too much to do for Alberta's number one cowboy to spend his time lying in bed.

But it was August 3rd before the doctors finally agreed to let Herman leave the hospital and go home. This was the longest time he had ever spent in a hospital and he was anxious to get going again. On August 21st, he made his usual trip to the Claresholm Stampede, not as arena director this time, but as a spectator.

Writing in the *Calgary Albertan,* the late Tommy Primrose took note of this unusual event with a story headlined: "Linder Sits Out This Rodeo," and went on to say: "Only recently returned to his ranch at Cardston after serious injuries, July 8th while arena director at the Fort Macleod Stampede, the famous rodeo cowboy and rodeo producer-rancher was almost his usual jaunty self again. For many years arena director at the Claresholm Stampede, Mr. Linder had his place taken this year by Reg Kessler of Rosemary. The two walked together to the center of the infield to be introduced and received tremendous applause from a packed grandstand, the infield cowboys and officials."

As Herman left for Expo, newspaper headlines and subheads said: "French Beret Replaces Stetson — Canada's Mr. Rodeo, Herman Linder of Cardston, Traded His Usual Western Stetson for a French Beret Saturday Prior to His Forthcoming Trip to Expo Where he will Produce a Western Rodeo."

He was still a bit stiff from his Fort Macleod accident but he was mending rapidly. And the success of the show was a potent tonic to a rodeo promoter who had often seen his best efforts go down the drain because of circumstances beyond his control. He even had quite a bit of expense money left over after he had paid all the bills. When he tried to give it back he was told people just didn't do things like that. But he gave it back anyway. There is no record of any official suffering a heart attack at the effrontery of anyone trying to give back Expo expense money, but it must have given some of them a nasty turn.

The only trouble with holding an October rodeo is that the weather is liable to play tricks on you and this time it did. There was also a transit strike on, which made it hard to get around the city. But that didn't deter the Montreal crowds from getting out to the show. There were never less than 10,000 people in the stands and the show made money.

"It's hard to say how much more we would've made if the weather had been good," said Herman. "I don't think I've ever been so cold at a rodeo. How those people came there day after day and sat until the whole show was over sure beats me. Usually, when it comes to bull riding, which is generally the last thing we put on, most people are ready to go home after they've seen one or two bulls. But these people stayed right to the end. It was really gratifying to me, I can tell you."

Mrs. Linder says it was one of the nicest and smoothest-running shows she ever attended, in spite of the miserable, blustery weather. Even the transit strike didn't bother her too much. "The roads were full of people trying to get out to the show," she said, "but at that time you never saw an empty car or cab. Everybody that had a vehicle picked people up off the street and took them out."

Herman's one big regret about Expo is that his mother didn't live to see him stage it. She died in 1960, forty-two years after she had come with her husband and family to make a home in this big land below the mountains.

CHAPTER FIFTEEN

FINAL GO ROUND

The walls of Herman's den are of varnished knotty pine overlain by an astonishing array of pictures of scenes and friends of his forty years in rodeo. There are pictures of well-known movie stars, of big-name rodeo riders, of the ships that took him and his cohorts across the seas. There are pictures of Herman perched on the hurricane deck of heaving broncs, being made an Indian chief, and sitting between Queen Elizabeth (then a Princess) and former Calgary Mayor Don MacKay, along with Prince Philip, as they watched a special stampede staged for the Royal couple.

And as you look, you marvel at the distance this man has travelled since he and his brother, Warner, first started to fool around with a horse that loved to buck named Pardner. Herman will tell you that Pardner almost discouraged him completely from ever becoming a bronc rider. But somehow you doubt that this would have happened because the record tells a very different story. It shows a man of stamina and courage, who was stimulated by challenge and always prayed he would draw the toughest horse and the unridable bull. The record says this man, Linder, had subconsciously decided what he wanted to be a long time ago — maybe as he looked out of the window of the Cahoon Hotel as a boy in Cardston that first night in the spring of 1918, listening to the jangle of harness and the music of horses' hooves. It says this is a born horseman, a natural rider destined to follow such a career.

You wonder about the changes that have taken place in rodeo itself in its years of evolving from a simple test of practical range skills to a multi-million-dollar sport that is now attracting city-bred youngsters into its ranks who learn their skills in special rodeo schools. And you wonder why some men can ride bucking horses and others cannot, no matter how hard they try or how much experience they have had on the range. Herman believes champions are born, not made, because the action is too swift for deliberate responses.

"It has to be in your reflexes," he said. "You don't have time to think what you're doing, or what you are going to do. Schools can save you a lot of time by teaching you some of the tricks of the trade we had to learn the hard way," he added, "but no amount of schooling can help if your reflexes are slow."

Do riders experience fear before a contest? Linder says that he never felt fear, just tension. And if he didn't feel that tension, he generally chalked up a pretty poor ride.

"Sometimes I'd go in and it was just like sitting in a rocking chair," he said, "no tension at all. In rides like that I found it was hardly worthwhile waiting around to learn my score. You've got to have that tension to tone up your muscles."

Why are so many non-ranch boys going in for a sport that was once the preserve of ranch people? Herman says the big drawback to ranch youngsters developing their rodeo skills is a lack of good bucking horses. Having horses to break and train once gave the ranch hand an advantage over any other would-be contestants. But ranches no longer keep the big strings of horses they used to have. Like the "Old Cowhand from the Rio Grande, who rides the range in a Ford V-8", a lot of work is now done with vehicles, even airplanes. Horses are kept for special tasks and often travel to a job in the back of a truck or trailer to save time.

"The bucking stock situation is changing a lot of things in rodeo," said Herman. "There aren't so many good bucking horses around, so the contractors try to save them and keep them bucking as long as possible. You can go to a rodeo show where there might not be more than nine or ten saddle broncs ridden, while it wasn't uncommon for us to have twenty-five to thirty saddle broncs ridden in one afternoon. I know when I rode in Lethbridge and Cardston we rode at least fifty head of bucking horses, bareback and saddle broncs, in an afternoon."

Herman figures the best bucker is a combination between a draft horse and a thoroughbred, rather than the range bronc. That combination gives a horse more weight and adds more zip to your ride, in his opinion.

One change for the better is that each rider now has his own saddle and the bareback contestants have their own special rigging.

"The saddles are now built a little like what we used to call a 'form-fitter' model," he said. "They aren't at all like the saddles we had back in those days. As for the bareback rigging, that has changed a lot too. Some of them used to have a handhold so big you could almost put your head through and if you wanted to put a handkerchief in there to take up some of the slack, the judges would disqualify you. They wouldn't even let you put resin on your gloves or on your chaps. In Calgary, they had a chute judge to see you didn't use anything like that on your equipment. In fact, they wouldn't let you take a wrap with a loose rope. But that's all been done away with. The Association has changed all that. It's pretty nice for the boys now."

Back in the days of the first stampedes, the kind of saddle you used might even decide whether or not you won a championship. Rules for the "Cowboy Bucking Horse Riding Contest With Saddle" found in an old program pasted in one of Herman's scrapbooks included a rule that "there shall be three judges and that their decision shall be final. Riders must ride slick saddle. Fork of the saddle can be any old width. No bucking rolls, quirts or whips will be allowed. Should the judges find that two riders have ridden equally well in all other respects, they will be instructed to give their decision in favor of the rider whose saddle has the narrower fork." This was years before the Linders even came to Alberta.

Herman thinks one of the best changes has been the use of experienced riders as judges. They have judging schools today which show films and instruct the judges on exactly what to look for, and how to mark the rides. Rodeo riding is so much better today there is just no comparison, he says. And the seeds of these improvements were planted back in Boston in 1936 when the boys staged their big strike against Colonel Johnson.

Herman doesn't think the public will give up on rodeo because of charges that it is cruel to animals. They might as well talk about stopping boxing matches and wrestling bouts, he says, for a bucking horse or rodeo steer takes a lot less of a beating than a boxer. They even lead much better lives than the average horse or cow.

"Wonderful care is taken of them," said Herman, "and with very good reason. They're valuable animals and becoming harder and harder to get. Buckers are used only about twice a week for ten seconds each ride. They get the best of feed, and when not working in a rodeo, they're turned out to pasture. Cattle are also used for only a few days a year and from one to sixty seconds each time. The stock has to be kept as fit as athletes who enter the sport world.

"As for calf throwing, it's like throwing men. They fight and kick, but it doesn't hurt them. It's no worse than roping them by a hind leg and dragging them to a branding fire."

The Linder Ranch may have been financed from the deck of a heaving bronc, but over the years it has developed into a solid, down-to-earth operation. From the start, it was run as a cow-calf enterprise using Hereford cattle as the main breeding. Then Herman and Agnes expanded into a feedlot for finishing commercial beef. They gave this up when son, George, who had obtained a B.Sc. in Agriculture at the University of Alberta, decided he wanted to come back to the ranch and raise exotic cattle.

George took an A.I. course and then tried his hand at breeding Simmental, Limousin, and Maine Anjou cattle. He bred ten cows to each of these exotics before finally settling on Maine Anjou as the breed he preferred to raise. Today, George is president of the Canadian Maine-Anjou Association and has made four trips to France to obtain new breeding stock. On the three occasions he couldn't go, Herman went in his place. In 1971, the Alberta government recognized the contributions of this family to their area and gave them a Master Farm Family Award.

The only Linder family member showing any desire to compete in rodeo was daughter, Rose Marie, a registered nurse, who competed in several barrel racing events. Rose Marie is now the wife of rodeo champion Tom Bews.

Herman got out of active rodeo in 1969 — 40 years after that first official win on Yellow Fever. But it's doubtful if rodeo ever got completely out of Herman. You can still find him at the National Rodeo finals in Oklahoma each year and, except for that time when he was badly hurt at the Fort Macleod rodeo, he has never missed a Calgary Stampede.

"It's something that's still in my blood, I guess," he admitted. "It's my first love, you might say."

And the rodeo world feels the same way about him. In 1975 he was given the honor of leading a team comprised of the top Canadian riders of 1974 to compete at the first international contest between the Number One riders of Canada and the United States, which was held at Pueblo, Colorado, during the summer. Heading the American team was Herman's old friend and fellow bronco busting champion, Casey Tibbs. It was a stand-off as far as the broncs were concerned: the Canadian boys won the Saddle Bronc event and the Americans came away with the Bareback title. They also won the Bull Riding.

But for Herman, the real thrill was being back in the rodeo game once more, hearing the old sounds and breathing the excitement of the contest.

INDEX

Tibbs, Casey, 106,123
Thompson, Don, 84
Too Bad, 4
Truitt, Dick, 84
Tucson, Arizona, 85
27 Bay, 88

University of Alberta, 122
Utledge, Don, 31

Vancouver, B.C.,
 6,34,75,91,96-109,113
Vancouver News Herald, 101
Vancouver Province, 101,104
Vancouver Sun, 100
Visalia, Cal., 17

Washington, D.C., 48
Waterton-Glacier National
 Parks, 15
Watmough, Ron, 95

Watrin, Slim, 28,31
Weadick, Guy, 13,34
Welch, Pete, 94
Weyman, Dorothy G., 63,64
Whiskey Roan, 88
White City Stadium, 56
Whiteman, Hub, 81
Wickenburg, Arizona, 85
Wilbur, Washington, 99
Windsor, Ontario, 47
Wister, Owen, 64
Wolff, Mrs. George, 45
Woll, Strawberry Red, 94
Wood, Marty, 115
World's Fair, 6,41

Yellow Fever, 17,88,89,123

Zeller, Agnes, 45
Zumalt, Oral, 72

CLIFF FAULKNOR

Cliff Faulknor was born, raised and educated in Vancouver, British Columbia. Upon completing high school he worked at various occupations across Canada, including millhand, assistant forest ranger, and harvester.

During World War II, Faulknor served as a marine diesel engineer on an army transport vessel. In 1945, he commenced classes at the University of British Columbia, graduating in 1949 with a Bachelor of Science in Agriculture degree. He then spent five years as a land inspector with the British Columbia Department of Lands and Forests, Division of Land Utilization Research and Survey. In 1954, he accepted a position as associate editor of *Country Guide* magazine, from which he retired in 1975. During this time he was a contributing editor to *Cattlemen* magazine in Calgary, where he maintained a close contact with the cattle industry.

Cliff Faulknor is the author of two adult books, six novels for juveniles and many short stories. He won his first short story contest while still in high school, and his book, *The White Calf,* winner of the Little, Brown Award, was published in four countries and made into a play for CBC radio. Most recently, he received the Alberta Culture award for the best nonfiction book by an Alberta author published in 1976, for his book *Pen and Plow.* At present, he lives in Calgary with his wife Betty, who types most of his manuscripts. They have a son and a daughter living in Alberta.

Herman Linder bought many of Bruce Cressmans top bucking Horses